GOVERNORS STATE UNIVERSITY LIBRARY

3 1611 00069 6648

P9-CFU-753

NOV 11 1985

Qânâq

Grise Fiord

BAFFIN BAY

GREENLAND

Nanisivik
Arctic Bay   Pond Inlet

Clyde River

Iglooolik
Hall Beach

Broughton Island

MELVILLE PENINSULA

Fox Basin

Pangnirtung

BAFFIN ISLAND

Repulse Bay

Frobisher Bay

Cape Dorset

Lake Harbour

Coral Harbour

LABRADOR SEA

Asbestos Hill

Ivujivik   Sugluk   Wakeham Bay   Port Burwell
                      Koartak

Ungava Bay   Saglek Bay
Payne Bay   Short Lake   Raman   Napartok Bay
Akulivik   George River   Hebron   Nutak   Tasiuyak Bay
                             Okak
Povungnituk   Korok River   Voisey Bay
        Leaf Bay   George River   Nain
HUDSON BAY   Fort Chimo   Davis Inlet
                         Hopedale   Makkovik
Port Harrison   Postville   Rigolet

NORTHERN QUEBEC   LABRADOR

                North West River
        Happy Valley

Sanikiluaq
Belcher Islands   Richmond Gulf

Great Whale River

James Bay

DATE DUE

JAN 0 2 1986			
	JAN 0 2 1986		
	NOV 30 1987		
	JUN 1 7 1997		
	APR 0 4 2000		

DEMCO NO. 38-298

INUIT
The North in Transition

by Ulli Steltzer

UNIVERSITY LIBRARY

GOVERNORS STATE UNIVERSITY

PARK FOREST SOUTH. ILL.

The University of Chicago Press

The University of Chicago Press, Chicago 60637
Douglas & McIntyre Ltd., Vancouver, British Columbia

© 1982 by Ulli Steltzer

All rights reserved. Published 1982
University of Chicago Press edition 1985

94 93 92 91 90 89 88 87 86 85   5 4 3 2 1

Library of Congress Cataloging in Publication Data

Steltzer, Ulli.
  Inuit, the North in transition.

  1. Eskimos—Canada. I. Title.
E99.E7S824 1985   971'.00497   84–23935
ISBN 0–226–77247–0 (pbk.)

TR
65

E 99 .E7 S824 1985

Steltzer, Ulli.

Inuit, the North in
  transition

For Renate

TR
65

E 99 .E7 S824 1985

Steltzer, Ulli.

Inuit, the North in
  transition

Contents

Acknowledgements

I want to thank the many people in the North who not only put me up but put up with me, fed me their delicious food, clothed me, hauled me safely over their land and waters, and talked to me freely and openly.

My deep appreciation goes to the following people and organizations: Michael Amarook of Inuit Tapirisat of Canada, who gave me his blessings for my project; Gunther Abrahamson of Indian and Northern Affairs in Ottawa, whose sensitive support and advice I have treasured; Canadian Arctic Producers and the Canadian Arctic Co-operative Federation, for inviting me twice to their meetings in Baffin Island; Tom Frook of Kenn Borek Air, who allowed me to cook, eat, live and fly with the pilots of Resolute Bay; Dome Petroleum Ltd., for transportation and two welcome meals at the Tuktoyaktuk base camp; Margaret and Tom Blom, for their caring friendship; Joseph Miller, who solved many of my editorial problems; Ted Masters, who during my absence took care of my house and garden, including the weeds; Horst Wenzel, in whose laboratory my cameras were successfully winterized. Last but not least I would like to thank Dr. Alfred Ernest Pallister of the Devonian Group of Charitable Foundations, who, by arranging the generous funding of my travels, gave the green light to go north.

Preface

Inuit have lived in the North for thousands of years under conditions of extraordinary physical hardship. To this day the Inuit hunters' strength and ability to endure cold and to survive on the frozen land is unsurpassed. But contact with the industrialized world has disrupted what was once a successful, if physically difficult, traditional way of life. The people no longer live year-round in camps, travelling freely over the land to hunt the animals that provided their food and clothing, tools and shelter. Encouraged by government, today's Inuit have settled permanently in communities close to schools, stores, nursing stations and other services. The wage economy is gradually making its way into the North, and even the smallest settlements offer jobs to their inhabitants, who have become increasingly dependent on imported food, household goods and clothing. In order to afford a snowmobile and gasoline, the hunter may find it necessary to seek a part-time job or take up carving as a means of earning income. The whole mercantile system is in opposition to the hunting society.

The strong cultural influences of the South as well as the encroachment of hydro projects and mineral and oil exploration are causing the Inuit anxiety about the future of their land and their culture. As a result, they have formed various political and cultural organizations which are working intensely towards solutions to such vitally important problems as land claims, wildlife management and language training. The complex, constantly changing affairs of government, though beyond the full understanding of most Inuit, affect all their lives. They are trying to respond on a day-to-day basis to every new move of government and industry.

This book is an attempt to give a realistic picture in photographs and the people's own words of Inuit today, not in theoretical or political terms, but in concrete, human terms — a picture of their daily lives, their pleasures and problems, their feelings about themselves and their environment. Because I wanted the Inuit to speak for themselves, the topics they discuss are for the most part of their own choosing, though my growing awareness of the issues at stake prompted me to seek out certain representative voices in the communities.

My original plan was to visit at least two communities in each of the six Arctic and sub-Arctic regions, but it was quickly apparent that this would not be adequate to cover such an enormous area. Over a period of a year and a half I spent twelve months in villages varying in size from fewer than a hundred people to nearly a thousand, travelling between the fifty-fifth and seventy-seventh parallels, from the Yukon border to Labrador, a distance greater than that from Moscow to Madrid. All this time I was photographing and listening and taking every opportunity to join the people on their hunting and fishing trips. For additional research, I relied on the book *Inuit Land Use and Occupancy Project* (Indian and Northern Affairs, 1976), which is based on information given by the Inuit themselves.

The northern landscape is as varied as it is vast. To be sure, the sea ice is flat, as is much of the land, and under a thick cover of snow Tuktoyaktuk might not look very different from Rankin Inlet. But each area does have its own distinct character: the pebble beach of Holman Island, the smooth rocky hills around Pelly Bay, the long lakes of the Keewatin backlands, the fiords and mountains of Baffin Island, the skinny trees of northern Quebec and Labrador, and the rocky islands of the Atlantic coast. The flora varies as much as the terrain, and during the short summer months a multitude of flowers and grasses, mushrooms, lichens and berries can be found. Even ice and snow change texture in different climates, seasons and light. In shocking contrast, the prefabricated houses, at least within the Northwest Territories, are everywhere identical. The latest models are certainly bigger and shinier than the old "matchbox" houses first built by the government, but they are just as unimaginative. Igloos, it may be argued, also look alike, but they are pleasing to the eye and fit perfectly into the landscape from which they are taken, as I discovered when we were out on the land. For to this day, the hunters of different regions build and use these sophisticated structures which vary from small temporary shelters to large underground buildings with side chambers, tunnels, porches, air vents, and windows of ice.

As a visitor in the Arctic, I was constantly discovering the differences in the small communities, but one overwhelming similarity bound together all my experiences: the generous hospitality of the people. Although I could usually book a scheduled flight, the remoteness of my destinations generally made it difficult to arrange sleeping accommodations ahead of time. I often felt awkward getting off a Twin Otter or a DC 3, facing all the people who had come to meet the plane and who knew or expected everybody but me. But as I stood surrounded by my bulky baggage — cameras, tripod, film, books, paper, tape recorder, sleeping bag, clothing — I was always greeted with warmth and invariably found some friendly person who was willing to haul me and my baggage from ice strip or air strip to the village, sometimes by truck, sometimes by snowmobile.

All my visits were open ended since it was impossible to predict events. A polar bear has to be hunted before you can take pictures of its skin being scraped or stretched. I must have been something of a novelty, since most white visitors work for the government in one way or another, stay overnight at the transient centre, and hurry away on the next plane. "For whom do you work?" people asked. "Are you the visiting nurse?

A teacher? How long are you here for?" I explained what I was trying to do, that I needed their help, and that I would like to stay until I was satisfied with my work.

In Igloolik, my first stop, Natalino Attagutaluk and his wife Catherine Arnatsiaq invited me to stay with them. They both had jobs: she worked as a clerk at the Hudson's Bay store and he drove the oil truck for the co-op, delivering heating oil to the houses. Natalino promised to take me seal hunting on the weekend. The night before we left, I was taken to his parents' house and dressed from top to toe in traditional caribou clothing. My down parka and pants were declared inadequate; so were my boots which I happily and permanently exchanged for soft, warm sealskin kamiks. The next morning it was forty below zero when we left. My camera case, a harpoon, Coleman stove, gun, gas cannister and I were loaded into a flat-bottomed wooden boat which Natalino had tied onto his father's big sled. Roped securely to the skidoo, the sled was pulled over six miles of sea ice out to the floe edge. It grew colder and colder as we approached the open sea. Other hunters joined us for a while; one of them stayed to help with the boat. Natalino shot a seal and his friend retrieved it from the water. I took pictures. The shutter of one of my cameras was frozen. So were my hands. Changing film was agony. I had learned my first lesson, and when, a week later, we went caribou hunting, I made sure never to take off my silk gloves. In time my hands healed, and I had my cameras properly winterized. Even so, when I brought them cold into the moist heat of a house, the condensation immediately froze into a sheet of ice over the lenses. The same was true for my glasses. I became used to missing a lot of good shots.

Just as the cold put limitations on my photographing, so the language barrier hampered my writing. At Pelly Bay I lived with Helen and Jacob Kringorn, both over seventy, neither of whom speaks a word of English. Helen, as is the custom, served tea as soon as I arrived. Then she summoned her granddaughter Beatrice to translate for us, and her first question to me was, "Where is your husband?" "He left me thirty years ago," I replied. Long pause. "Do you have children?" "Yes, two, and two grandchildren." Helen's eyes lit up: we had something in common. A lively and humorous old woman, she then proceeded candidly to tell me the story of her marriage to Jacob, after which Jacob told me about his youth. I wrote feverishly. But during the two weeks I lived with the Kringorns, this was the only real conversation we had. Beatrice, feeling used, made a point of disappearing whenever she thought herself in danger of being pressed into service again. I learned another lesson. I must not push too hard.

Some of my translators were very young and no doubt missed some fine detail of speech. This was not true of Elisabeth Banksland of Holman Island, who offered to translate her old mother's stories. And when I did not quite know how to start a conversation with Agnes Nigiyok, I finally told her that there was an empty page for her in the book I was making, that I would like to take her picture and write down any message she had for the people in the South. She said eagerly, "They camp on our land. They drive the caribou away. Tell them to stay home."

Perhaps my most revealing insight into translating Inuktitut came in Grise Fiord. Jopee, the leader of a singing group known as the Fiordics, was singing his own song to the guitar when I asked him for a translation. He tried. It was a song about Inuit hunting in the past by dog team and now by snowmobile. His English was good, and the content of the song seemed to be simple enough. We sat for two hours, but none of the English versions pleased him. "That's no longer my song," he finally said. "It's beautiful in Inuktitut; it sounds all wrong in English."

I thought often of Jopee's comment, for the problem of communication is a serious one in the North. In Labrador and the western Arctic, where there has been longer contact with white people, English is spoken in every home by the younger generations, but often children cannot understand their Inuktitut-speaking grandparents. In northern Quebec where the schools teach some children in French and some in English, Inuktitut remains the only shared language and is spoken by everybody. There in Povungnituk, a group of young children greeted me: "Bonsour!" I said, "Bonjour!" One little girl asked, "Kinauvit?" I answered, "Ulli." The little girl replied, "Ullingay!" and I acknowledged her greeting with the long "Ay" sound that politeness requires. They looked at me. All of a sudden they took off like a flock of birds, calling "Bye! Bye! Bye!" How much I regret not knowing more than a few phrases of the different Inuktitut dialects (Inuktut in Labrador); of many conversations I could make out only soft and pleasing sounds.

One weekend in April, when I tried to reach George River by telephone, not a single family answered. My hostess in Fort Chimo guessed right, that the entire village had moved to Short Lake to fish. By Easter everybody was back in town for a week of games, races and square dances. These activities were taken seriously and enjoyed just as much as the fishing or the ptarmigan hunting. All over the Arctic, communities get together for summer games, winter games and spring games. I missed many of these, though in planning my travels I tried to be in the right places at the right times: Grise Fiord for the polar bear season, Sachs Harbour for fox trapping, Holman Island for the seal hunt. But no matter where I went, I was told: You should have been here last week when the capelin washed ashore . . . You should stay till the geese are coming . . . You should see this place in summertime!

As good as I felt about the warm welcome given me everywhere in the North, I felt as sad when I had to say good-bye. "Phone us sometime," my new friends said. "Write to us. Tell us if you want something." After three weeks in Grise Fiord I told Tookillkee Kiguktak that I had to leave as soon as there was a plane. He said, "I hope the weather stays bad for a long, long time. Once you go away, you will never come back." The next day he took me to the plane and without saying a word, he turned away and walked back to his snowmobile.

The photographs and text in the following pages are the result of the trust and co-operation I received from the people in the North. For a while there our heartbeats were the same. With this book I return to the Inuit what I was given: an insight into their lives which they so generously shared.

Baffin Island and the High Arctic

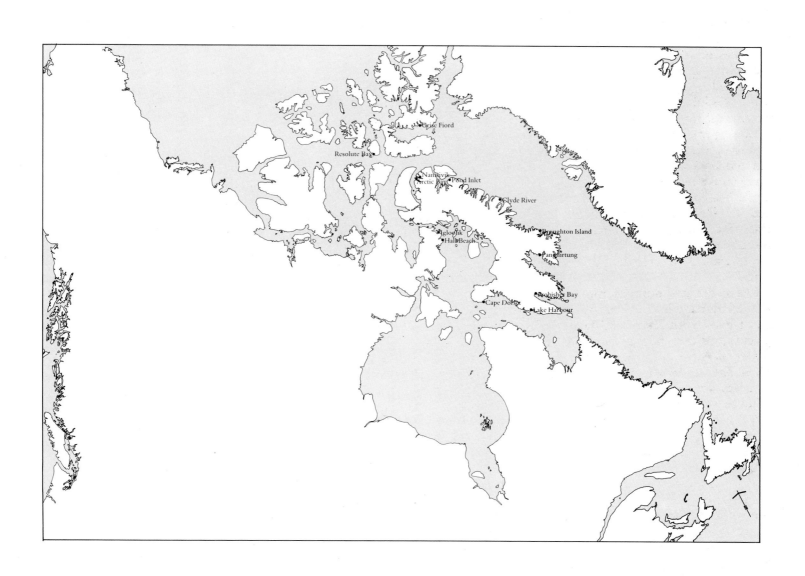

Grise Fiord

Resolute Bay

Nanisivik
Arctic Bay • Pond Inlet

Clyde River

Igloolik
Hall Beach

Broughton Island

Pangnirtung

Frobisher Bay
Cape Dorset • Lake Harbour

*Natalino Attagutaluk uses his harpoon to test the new ice at the floe edge. At Igloolik by March the ice
has formed six miles out from the land.*

See the smoke over the water. It is there only when it's real cold. The water
moves fast every six hours. That's why it doesn't freeze over.
Natalino Attagutaluk, Igloolik

Natalino waits for the seal to surface.

While his friend retrieves the seal, Natalino stands ready to pull the boat onto the ice.

Natalino makes tea while his friend cleans out the seal.

Natalino's son Christopher, known as "Sunny Boy"

We like our kids to play outside and our people to work. That's why we don't have TV in Igloolik. And we don't have much liquor; it's too many troubles.

Catherine Arnatsiaq, Igloolik

Michel Kopak, Natalino's father

The ice is the same every year, but the water makes different forms on it. When you are coming home from hunting and it blows and the weather is bad, you could get lost. We can tell from the snow how to get home, from the way the wind makes the snow look. And we can tell from the forms the water makes on the ice how to get home. In the summertime it is easy; we can tell by the rocks—even the little ones.

This land has always been ours. Now the governments say it belongs to them. You take one of them, maybe Trudeau, and you put him on the land and he doesn't know where to go, and he doesn't know what to do. Maybe if you give him a compass he can find Igloolik, maybe not. That's why I say, this is our land.

Michel Kopak, Igloolik

Ice formations

Snow formations

Susan Avingaq tends her kuliq (seal oil lamp) with a takut (a soapstone tool)

I built myself a little house away from the big house to work on my caribou skins. It is made of wood and skins. I call it an igloo. If it were made of snow, I would call it an igluviak. Sometimes I sleep in it. I like the old ways.

We use all kinds of fat for the kuliq [seal oil lamp]. When we have seal fat, we use that; it melts better. In the summertime when we go to the land, we find the little plants that look like cotton balls. We use them for wicks. The kuliq gives the light and the heat.

Susan Avingaq, Igloolik

I like carving better than working for somebody because I get more money for it, but I often get tired of it.

Sometimes I can't get stone for a long time, when the co-op does not have any. There is stone around here and north on Baffin Island. We used it in the past, but it is too hard to carve and too hard to mine. There is better stone in the south of Baffin Island. The one I am carving now is from Lake Harbour.

Lukie Airut, Igloolik

Augustin and Theresia Taqqaugaq, carvers, enjoy working together.

Morning recess at the Attagutaluk school

We are always breaking new ground up here in Igloolik. For example, we do most of the teaching in our first three grades in Inuktitut. As far as local control in education is concerned, we are a lot more advanced than some other communities in the Northwest Territories. Next year we will have eleven Inuit teachers from Igloolik and eight teachers from the south. The aim of the community is to have the children learn more traditional skills. That will probably mean less social studies and sciences.

Our school goes to grade nine. That's usually the end of formal education. We have very few kids who go away to Frobisher Bay for schooling—maybe two or three a year. And the numbers who stay to graduate are even smaller. Only two people from here have gone to college.

We would like to get certified Inuit teachers, but so far there aren't any. I can not pass on the Inuit cultural tradition; no southern teacher can. All we can pass on is our own tradition, our southern white values, and of course they don't fit here. Whatever blending of the two cultures there is should be of the Inuit's choosing, not the government's, as it was before we had organized local initiative. Igloolik people should have the balance of education they want. These are *their* children.

Jack Waye, principal of the Attagutaluk School, Igloolik

John Maurice's Grade 6 science class.
John Maurice: Liver, liver, this is the liver; L-I-V-E-R.
Student: It's good. I like it.

The guests at this birthday party are looking forward to a mitt-matching race.

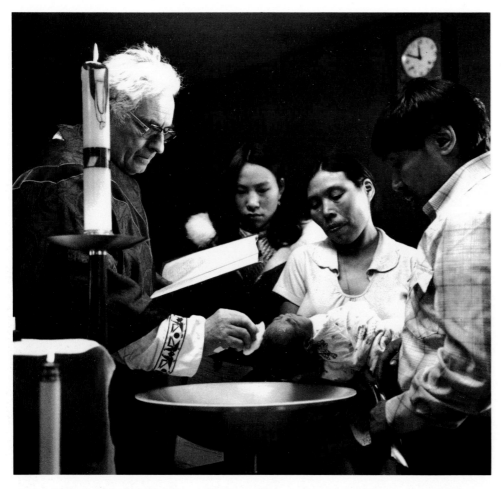

Father Robert Lechat, baptizing Kateri, daughter of Antonin Qrungnut and Leonie Arnagalak

When I was a baby, the priest from the ship wanted to baptize an Inuk. I was the only one available at that time. He named me Michelline. I don't like it; it's too long. The old people can't even pronounce my name. But that's the way it used to be. The priest would choose any name he wanted.

I have nine Inuit names, but I use only one of them. When I have children, I will be the one to choose the Christian name. All Inuit names are given by the old people.

Michelline Ammaq, Igloolik

Inuit are starting to use the family name for the women and even the children. Before, the government just gave them a number.

In the old days the Christian names were chosen by the missionary and, depending on where the priest came from, the names were English, French, Flemish, or even Italian. That's how Natalino and Michelline got their names.

Inuit names are passed on. As soon as a person dies, that name is given to a child by the old people. The person's title [family relationship] also goes with that name. For example, a baby is given the name of its grandfather; it may then be called Father by its parents and may in turn call its father, Son. But there is more that goes with that name. It is a kind of reincarnation. You have to be nice to the child so you don't hurt its spirit; otherwise, you are in trouble. I remember when a young person died, eleven people asked for that name. It was their way to pacify that spirit.

Father Robert Lechat, OMI, Igloolik

I have ten children but gave two of them for adoption, one to a relative and one to a friend. If our relatives want our children, they could have them. The children are happy that way.

Marie Airut, Igloolik

When we had our second boy, we gave it to my aunt. She wanted a boy real bad and never had one so she adopted him. I wanted a girl anyway.

Attagutaluk was the Queen of Igloolik. It is a very old name. It was Nat's great-grandmother's name and was given to Nat as a second name when he was a baby. That's the way we do it. Somebody dies and the name goes to a baby, it does not matter whether it is a boy or a girl.

Catherine Arnatsiaq, Igloolik

Natalino Attagutaluk

Marie Airut visits with Noah Piugattuk while he is working on his fish nets.

Sometimes I like living in a house, sometimes I don't like it. I am making a net for catching baby seals in springtime. I am going out on the land maybe for a month and that is when I am going to use this net.

I like hunting caribou beside the lake because I like to watch when there are many of them. Sometimes I just watch them going wherever they go. That's why I like hunting caribou in the summertime.

The song of a man who goes out on the land and has a hard time when he is hunting:

    I want to find a caribou.
    Even if I see a big rock
    I will be happy that I see a caribou.

The song of a man who goes out on the ice and has a hard time finding a seal:

    I want to find a seal.
    Even if I see a big rock
    I will be happy that I see a seal.

Noah Piugattuk, Igloolik

Caribou at Melville Peninsula

Natalino examines the caribou he has shot.

There is no other place for us to earn money, and we enjoy working here. We make all the different clothes that people need. We make them out of caribou skin and sealskin and duffel: slippers, mittens, parkas, kamiks [boots], and socks to go inside the kamiks. What we make here, we sell. What we make at home, we make for the family.

Jeanie Arnainut, Arnait Katujiqatiriit (Women's Craft Shop), Igloolik

Natalino skins the caribou while it is still warm.

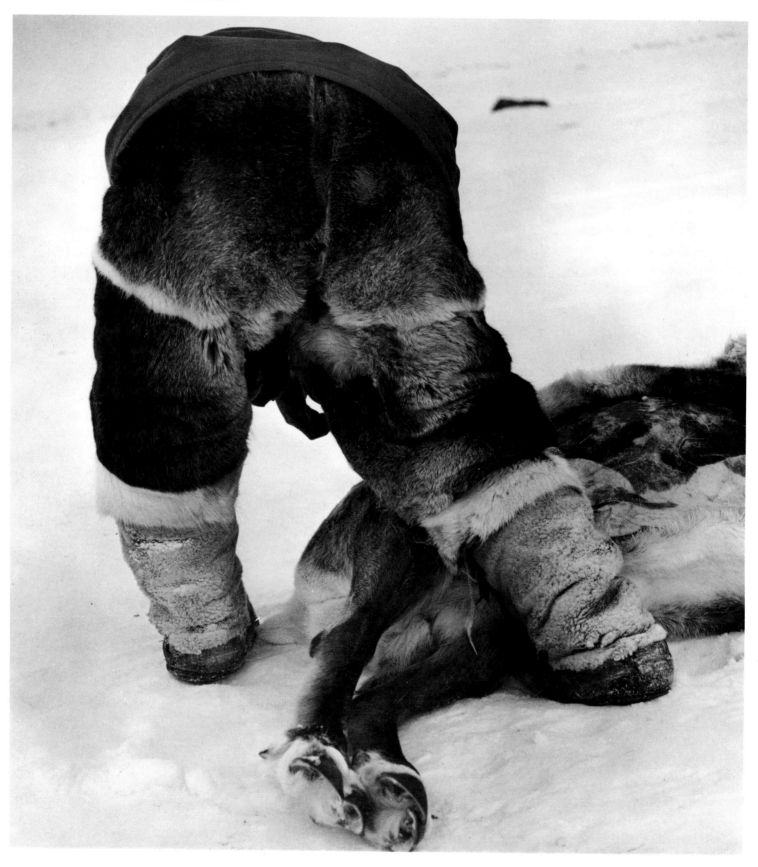

Jeanie Arnainut, chewing the stiff caribou hide to soften it

Yvonne Paniaq, sewing a caribou parka at the Arnait Katujiqatiriit.

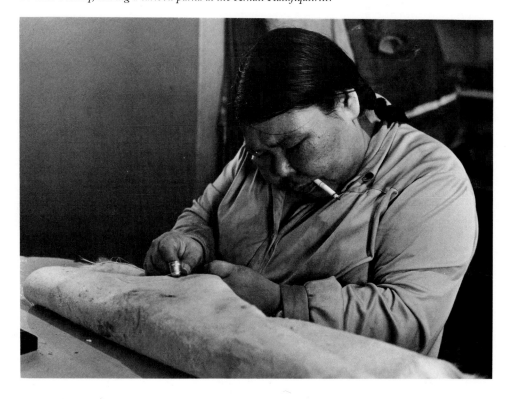

A team of twenty-six dogs, home from a trip to Baffin Island. With very few exceptions, hamlet and settlement councils require all dogs except puppies to be tied up.

Not too many years ago I had all white dogs with spots. Some teams were all black, some all brown. Now only six families have dog teams and the colours are all mixed.

Every dog gets trained, and we give every dog a name, but one dog has to be the leader, just like Inuit.

I feed the dogs every second day when I use them. They walk too slowly when they are skinny. We can tell by their fur when they have good meat. When they travel, they get fed every day, morning or night, it doesn't matter. We hunt for their food on the way. It is safer to hunt with dogs, but very slow.

When we started to use skidoos, a lot of dogs starved. We were too busy having fun running around with our skidoos.

Natalino Attagutaluk, Igloolik

As soon as the sea freezes over, the community of Grise Fiord expands onto the ice.

My wife is related to some people from Qânâq, Greenland. Sometimes in spring they come over by dog team. It takes them eleven days and they might stay a week or so. We are all happy together. Then they go back. On their way home they hunt for polar bear.

The Greenlanders wear polar bear pants and caribou parkas. The women's kamiks are up to their hips. They are made from sealskin with rabbit fur inside—real warm. Greenlanders never sell polar bear skins. They only shoot what they need themselves for clothing.

We went twice on a charter plane to Greenland. There were twenty-five of us and twenty-five Greenlanders came here. Then the plane picked them up again and brought us back. Like an exchange.

Once Simon Akpaleeapik and Nigiuk Kilukti went over by skidoo.

Tookillkee Kiguktak, Grise Fiord

Tookillkee Kiguktak, finishing off his igloo

Jimmy Nowra cuts ice from an iceberg that provides drinking water for the community. Being of glacial origin, it contains no salt.

The ice is cut and hauled into individual houses where it melts in big plastic containers.

Easter Sunday, Grise Fiord

Easter feast at the community hall. The menu: frozen caribou

There is a great difference between the way an Inuk thinks and the way a qallunaaq [white person] thinks. I am sort of in between. I could go either way. Sometimes that is difficult.

It is easier to talk about feelings to a qallunaaq or to an English-speaking Inuk. There are more words in the English language to express feelings. Most of the older Inuit just say what they think, not what they feel.

Sometimes being Inuk is really free. We don't grow up with a lot of rules. Our parents don't get mad when we make a mistake; they just help us and teach us.

Joanna Kiguktak, lay dispenser at the nursing station, Grise Fiord

Joanna Kiguktak and her daughter Jeannie, eating muktuk (frozen beluga whale skin)

Anna and Lucie Nungaq, combing the down from musk ox fur. The down is scarce and of great commercial value, being softer and warmer than cashmere.

My father made my tools. He could make ulus out of bone. I use the ulu for sealskin scraping, for cutting meat, cutting out the caribou parka, cutting out the sealskins to make kamiks, and to take out the fat from musk ox and polar bear. If I did not have an ulu, I would not make anything. The rounded tools are used to make the skins soft; the straight one, to take the fur off the sealskin for making kamiks. The skin of the bearded seal that we use for soles needs to be chewed to make it soft. I can't do it any more; I chewed too many.

Martha Kiguktak, Grise Fiord

Martha Kiguktak's tools

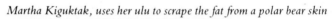

Martha Kiguktak, uses her ulu to scrape the fat from a polar bear skin

When you go seal hunting in the dark season, you look for certain formations in the snow. That is how you find the breathing holes. Usually there is twilight or there are stars and the moon. Even if there is no light I go hunting—I just get on the skidoo, turn on the lights and follow the bear tracks

The mother bear walks around with her cubs all winter to feed them and keep them from freezing. The male goes denning in November. If he is fat when he goes denning, he is still fat when he gets moving again in March.

Simon Akpaleeapik, Grise Fiord

The frozen remains of nanuq, the polar bear

Gamaliel and Ooleesee Akeeagok and Odlosiovik Nutarajuk, stretching a polar bear skin

A drying polar bear skin

It was the short Hudson's Bay manager from Pond Inlet, with a big wife, and the RCMP who asked them to come here. Akpaleeapik and Arnakallak were to stay in Grise Fiord for three years to teach the people, who had come from Port Harrison, how to hunt in the dark.

July fifteenth, 1953, we left Pond Inlet with the *C.D. Howe*. Even though there was lots of ice, the ship went ahead. It was much colder than in Pond Inlet when we got here.

Arnakallak went back after the three years because of his grandmother, who could still walk slowly if you helped her to stand up.

The young people today are different from what we were. They don't help old people and people who can't do things by themselves. Here everybody comes from different places and they have different ways of doing things. Maybe that's why the young people are like that.

Tatega Akpaleeapik, Grise Fiord

Tatega Akpaleeapik

34

Joseph Flaherty, son of Robert Flaherty the filmmaker

I can ask my sister to wash the floor. She'll do it. I can ask her anything. She'll do it.

If my parents ask me to do something, I'll do it. If my father tells me to go get a seal, I go.

My brothers, they are like that. We all are like that.

Jopee Kiguktak, Grise Fiord

Sometimes I watch movies all night. What else is there to do when the nights are long?

The settlement manager from Resolute sends movies up here—video tape. Three dollars a movie. We play them over and over again till the next plane comes in, maybe a week or two; by then we can hardly wait for new ones.

There have to be four or five hundred people in the settlement before you can get real TV. No way we can get it with only ninety-three people in Grise Fiord.

Charlie Noah, Grise Fiord

You could get trapped on the ice when it breaks up. Dogs know how to get around it, but with the skidoo it is dangerous. In Port Harrison the ice goes away altogether in the summertime; here it never goes away.

It would be better to have dogs if you went hunting all the time. It is easy to feed them. But if you have a job and you go hunting only after work and on weekends, you are better off with a skidoo. We always keep some dogs around for fur, to make parkas, or for pets for the kids.

Simon Akpaleeapik, Grise Fiord

Simon Akpaleeapik, while visiting in Resolute Bay, makes a qamutik (sled) out of boards salvaged from crates. It will serve to take tourists from Resolute Bay to Grise Fiord.

Interrupted sled ride in Lake Harbour

Pangnirtung

Arctic Bay

Mother and child at the sewing shop in Arctic Bay

We buy fur from the hunter and send it out for auction in Vancouver, B.C.

Hunters and Trappers is a membership association. Here hunters can buy their equipment for lower prices and sell fur for higher prices than elsewhere locally. We sell anything from skidoos to tents and Coleman stoves.

There is no quota for fox. The polar bear quota for Arctic Bay is sixteen a year. The government sets both the quota and the season.

Dave Campbell, secretary-manager for the local
Hunters and Trappers Association, Arctic Bay

The office of Arctic Bay's Hunters and Trappers Association

John Weetaltuk at Nanisivik Mines Ltd. The mine produces zinc and lead concentrates which are shipped out by boat during the summer months.

I surveyed at Queensway Highway in Ottawa where Canada Manpower sent me to train. Then Yellowknife, Hay River, Fort Smith, Fort Simpson. All that was surface survey. Now I do mostly underground survey. Drafting is part of it. I am updating maps and doing a lot of calculations.

Nanisivik means "place where things are found." Only men used to work here. We knew each other quite a bit. Now there are also women here. Most of them are employed at the site. My family is here too.

Today most of the married men live with their wives and there isn't much socializing any more. The workload is heavy: fifty-four hours a week for the men, forty hours for the women. When you get home, you stay home.

John Weetaltuk, surveyor and draftsman, Nanisivik

They have taken everything of the South and put it here to make living as comfortable as possible. This in one of the few communities in the North that has a sewer system. The others have honey bags. And we do have TV. I've certainly never regretted making the decision to come north.

Cynthia Rowan, Nanisivik Mines employee, Nanisivik

To be able to broadcast a half hour program twice a week, we film four times a week and edit almost every day. We use video tape in the studio and around the community, but now we are ready to go out with a Super 8 camera and film in other settlements. In the springtime we film different kinds of hunting: seal, narwhal and polar bear. Pond Inlet has really started to like seeing their own people on television and hearing their own language.

Paul Kautainuk, Pond Inlet

Producers of Pic TV, in Pond Inlet, editing tapes of a film they made for the local Alcohol Education Committee

The Telesat receiver picks up the signal from the Anik satellite to broadcast CBC television and radio. It also picks up telephone calls for Pond Inlet.

Western Arctic

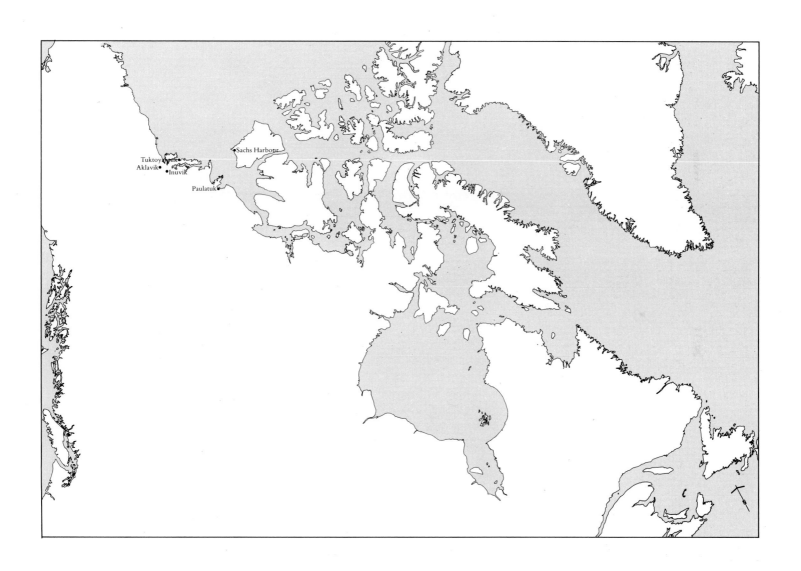

On the first day of snow, Hank Wolki shot a snowy owl.

We want to be careful with our land claims, not just sell out for cash. When we finally settle, it will be to protect our land and the animals that we need for our living.

Edward Ruben, Paulatuk

Billy Ruben, Paulatak

Liz and James Ruben live in a tent while waiting for the renovation of an old house.

There is no place where hunting is as easy as around here in the summer-time. You don't have to go after the caribou; they zigzag right down to the beach.

Edward Ruben, Paulatuk

That's why people like to stay here; they like to live off the land. Right now I haul gravel, but if it rains we can't work. It's only for the summer anyway. My job is to count how many caribou people hunt and to call Inuvik every day to tell them the weather. Everybody has little jobs, but it is not enough money. We need to hunt to feed our families.

If I got some meat and somebody needs it, they come and get a piece, and if I need some, I can go and get it. Nobody gets left out.

James Ruben, Paulatuk

In other places, when you want something you pay for it. Here you can still get something for nothing.

David Ruben, Paulatuk

This is a good place to live. We've got everything, and it is quiet unless they are flying the booze in. But even then it doesn't get out of hand; just loud music when they are partying. In 1959 we left here to move close to the DEW Line site at Cape Parry. There were a few jobs and there was a Hudson's Bay store. But there were not enough jobs and hunting was not so good.

When we reopened this settlement again in 1967, that's when we first had the RCMP come around. We were so scared of them. They were so big, they looked like moose and musk ox to us.

We still have very few white people come in here and if they come, they don't visit with us. They are in and out in a hurry.

Nora Ruben, Co-op clerk and agent for Kenn Borek Air Ltd., Paulatuk

Paulatuk in August

Father Leonce Dehurtevent

Three little Rubens get ready for supper.

Father stayed with us all the time. When we moved to Cape Parry, he moved with us. When we came back, he moved again. Always with us. Even in fish camp, he came out every week. He's part of our life. We've known him ever since we've been kids.

He says if he had the power to stop the airplanes in the air from bringing the booze in here, he would. Even though you do wrong, I don't think he'll ever mention anything. Never blame anybody but the devil.

Nora Ruben, Paulatuk

Why would I want to leave Paulatuk after so many years? This is where my work is, and I have to complete it.

The older I get, the happier I am. Wearing old clothes, it means nothing. Material things, they have no importance. A small settlement like this is just right for me, and after thirty years I like to think I have a share in this community.

Father Leonce Dehurtevent, OMI, Paulatuk

Father knows how to do many things. When a guy has to go trapping or fishing, father always takes his place. He looks after the power plant, he gives out the gas, and he looks after weighing and freezing the fish at the fish plant. And he teaches catechism too.

Mary Green, Paulatuk

Father, you know, he's a priest. They don't fight and they don't drink.

Josie Green, age seven, Paulatuk

Brenda Ruben: I like to rinse with Scope!
Frances Ruben: I rinse my mouth with Listermint.

Bertha Ruben: I have fifteen kids; lots of work to grow them up!

There is nothing but cousins in this town—cousins, uncles and aunties. The boys go out working for a while and bring back a girl. There should be some different families around. Out of a hundred and sixty people, seventy-two are Rubens.

Marlene Ruben, Paulatuk

The children love to swim, but even in summer a brief dip in the water is all a body can stand.

Evening at the Hornaday River fish camp. The men go twice a day to check their nets.

The char is sold commercially.

Family members take turns cleaning whitefish and Arctic char.

I take my wife to the store in Inuvik every six months or so. I tell her to buy anything she wants. When I see my family satisfied, I smile. What good is it to save the money?

When that first plane came in to Paulatuk, my youngest sister was alone in her house. She sees that plane and gets real scared. First thing, she covers her kids under a blanket; then she takes a gun to go after that plane.

Edward Ruben, Paulatuk

Edward and Mabel Ruben

After shooting a caribou, Edward Ruben and his son Chris take the skin and antlers back to camp. Because the animal was sick, its carcass was left behind.

I am not against development of the North, but we want to know what the oil companies are doing and where they are doing it. We have to live from this land; they don't. If they spill that oil, it will ruin everything we depend on.

Dome Petroleum is the only company that lets us know what they are doing. They have meetings with us all the time. They even show us movies of their operation. But we want to watch them too.

For seventeen years I worked on the DEW Line. There are new faces all the time, new rules, new bosses. "Ruben, you are a good man," one of them says to me; "Ruben, you are my best friend," says another one. He don't even know me. It's just talk; maybe I'm not a good man. Privileges are given and taken away. I got so disgusted, I finally quit.

Edward Ruben, Paulatuk

My grandfather said to me when I was little, "One of these days you can't depend on other people, you have to make a living for yourself; the animals won't come to your door, you have to go look for them."

Edward Ruben, Paulatuk

James Ruben, bringing back meat from Brock River

Brock River has driftwood—a rare commodity, rocks to weigh down the fish nets, and good caribou hunting.

When I saw all those straight lines in the pictures in books and in the movies, I thought they were making it up. Then I flew to Edmonton. Who would ever think of making those streets all straight and putting them trees all in one row, and even the flowers?

And when I was flying over the land and was looking down, up here it is just one big land, down there it is all in pieces like one big puzzle.

Mabel Ruben, Paulatuk

October is freeze-up time.

You get your plane all loaded with freight and your passengers waiting to leave, and the weather station tells you that Sachs Harbour is fogged in to the ground. There is no wind to move that stuff out of there. So you say, "See you tomorrow, folks." It's a hurry-up-and-wait situation so common to the North. Everyone here knows that type of delay and makes allowances for it.

When you have to do a medical evacuation, it gets more critical. Medivacs are a big part of our operation. We did about three hundred of them out of this base in one year, anything from newborn babies to major surgical cases. Some we bring to Inuvik hospital, others right down to Edmonton. In bad weather our pilots may expose themselves to outright danger. They are slow to accept defeat.

Greg Lang, base manager for Kenn Borek Air Ltd., Inuvik

The land is our life. The government says we don't own this land. They say the Eskimos are nomadic and don't stay in one place long enough to call it their own.

In government terms we don't own this land because we have nothing in writing. Our people did not write. When they made agreements, they trusted each other. All that was needed was a handshake.

For a long time our families camped in different places all around Banks Island during the trapping season. It is only recently that we have settled around the school in one community, but we are still hunting and trapping all over the island.

The economy of this community is based on trapping white fox. Beyond that, we think we have the best caribou in the world. If that were gone, I don't think the people would want to live here.

In the fifties and sixties the government sold the subsurface rights of Banks Island to some oil companies without consulting with us. They just called this crown land. These companies were already shipping their equipment across the Beaufort Sea before they started to talk with us. We were going to take them to court but instead settled for an agreement. We allowed them to work only during the winter months and made terms and conditions under which they had to do their work. To make sure that they went by our rules, we had monitors going along with their crew.

So far the companies have been pretty good, but we worry about what will happen if they actually find oil or minerals. Will they still respect our rules?

There have been big changes in the last years: housing, skidoos, transportation, communication. Still, we are hunters and trappers and we continue with our way of life.

Andy Carpenter, COPE (Committee for Original Peoples Entitlement)
negotiator for Sachs Harbour

Only two people in Sachs Harbour live in their own houses now. Both are single men. Everybody else has moved into government housing. The rising cost of fuel forced us out of our homes.

To me this doesn't make sense, but there is no subsidy for fuel if you have built your own house. Some good houses stand empty now. In government housing your fuel and electricity is paid for. You pay twenty-five per cent of your income for rent, but no less than twenty-eight dollars and no more than two hundred and fifty dollars.

All government houses are prefab. By the time they get here, they are often damaged or wet and don't fit together right. And if a house shifts a bit you get cracks, and the draft comes in.

It is hard to get parts for the cheap plastic bathrooms they put in. They may break twice a year. It would be cheaper for the government to give us good ones to start with.

We were independent as long as we owned our houses. We worked hard, but we were free. Now we are dependents of the government.

Peter Esau, president of the Housing Association, Sachs Harbour

Peter Esau with his sled load of caribou

Before going trapping, boys are required to fix and mark their traps.

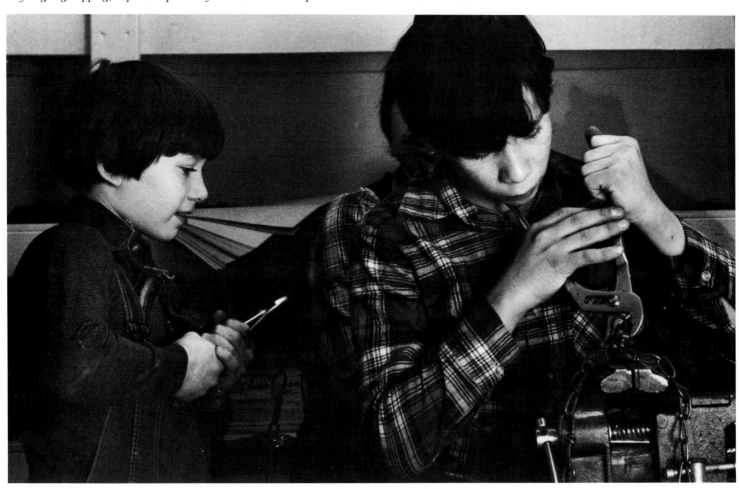

Christl, Thomas and Tina Carpenter

There is nothing between us and the wilderness—so many animals close by. Every year polar bears come to our beach, sometimes right into the settlement, even though there are big lights on the road. You watch every time the dogs start barking. And you watch where your kids go to play; you don't leave the little ones out of sight. A hungry bear will attack anything alive. I watched a bear right outside the house trying to get at the pups in the corral. Another bear chased Peter Esau. Peter couldn't make it to his house and jumped on his skidoo. First the bear went after the skidoo, then it killed Peter's dog—ripped the stomach right open. Quite a few dogs have been killed in the past. It's pure luck we haven't lost any kids so far.

Agnes Carpenter, Sachs Harbour

Lining up at the Inualthuyak School, Sachs Harbour

Ulukuluk Elias, a teacher of native crafts and a CBC reporter

Card game at the Eliases

Forty-two years ago today Noah and I went by dog team to get married. Our parents picked the spouse for us. That's just the way it was. I was only seventeen and Noah was nineteen. I didn't like being married at first until I started to love him. We have fifteen children, but you couldn't count our grandchildren.

Ulukuluk Elias, Sachs Harbour

Feast at the Eliases' wedding anniversary

Fred Carpenter, the first man to settle permanently in Sachs Harbour

I was only a little boy when the explorer Stefansson came to my mother's place, to that sod house my grandparents owned in the Tuk area. We were all sitting together on the floor, eating. Stefansson said to me, "Your mom and dad are Eskimo, how come you have blue eyes? I can tell you are a little bit white man." And he grabbed me and had me sit on his knees.

That was before Stefansson had started to map this island which the Eskimos called Igasuk.

Billy Banksland was Stefansson's guide for five years. It took the two men two or three years to map Igasuk. They went by dog team, but they walked every foot of the island all along the shore and into the river beds, and they measured every step. If Stefansson got tired, Billy walked ahead of the dog team. They also measured the island across.

Stefansson said, "Without Billy Banksland, the dogs and I would starve to death, but as long as Billy has one shot left I know I will live."

Stefansson called this island Banksland. The maps call it Banks Island.

Fred Carpenter, Sachs Harbour

People have come here a long time. They come by schooner in fall. They bring dog teams, sleds, coal, everything by schooner. They build frame tent, moss underneath to keep the dampness out, snow around the tent. 'On the trap line they build snow houses.

All that time it is blowing cold. No insulation. In summer people go back to the mainland. Next fall they come again, build a new tent.

I first come up here in 1930, work around the camp, going back to the mainland all the time. In 1938 I start trapping. After my husband is dead I go trapping with Michael Amos, and with my little girl all wrapped up.

Fred Carpenter is the first one to build a house here. I stay with him that time. I shoot polar bear in summer only. No law that time against shooting them in summer.

I have arthritis now. I have it bad. It is good to live in a house—warm.

Susie Sidney, Sachs Harbour

Susie Sidney, former hunter and trapper

Bill Seymour was white man from outside somewhere. He came with Stefansson on that boat that was called *Polar Bear*; he must have been his first mate, maybe.

Bill Seymour bought me from my adopted father when I was old enough to kill caribou with bow and arrow, maybe sixteen, seventeen. He paid one rifle, ten boxes of shells, one ulu, one saw, and he give him some clothes too.

Bill Seymour took me from Walker Bay to Herschel Island. That's where he lived. I work for him then. I stay with him many years. Until I am thirty, maybe. When I have TB, I learn a little bit in hospital, also from old Seymour. Never go to school. Later I get married and live all over the place.

Now we use rifle scope for hunting caribou. That way you can see really good. I am old for trapping but good for hunting.

William Kuptana, Sachs Harbour

When the police got here in 1954 they said to me, "Thanks, Fred, for holding this island for the Canadian government all these years." I laugh. "Good fox country, that's why I'm here."

Fred Carpenter, Sachs Harbour

You think we are lonely when we are out on the land. I tell you, it's the people in the city who are lonely.

Roger Kuptana, Sachs Harbour

Roger Kuptana, Joe Kudlak and Charles Elanik checking fox traps

Roger Kuptana, president of the Sachs Harbour Hunters and Trappers Association. Individual trap-lines can extend for 150 miles.

Before they can be skinned, the fox need to defrost.

Shirley Esau, cleaning the pelts with a special brush

Reindeer at the winter roundup

William Nasogaluak, owner of the only Canadian commercial reindeer herd

Reindeer are not native to Canada; the first North American herd was brought from Siberia to Alaska in the early nineteen hundreds. In 1929, the herd's Alaskan owners agreed to sell the Canadian government a herd of three thousand reindeer to supplement the dwindling wildlife in the Mackenzie River delta area. A Laplander, Andrew Bahr, was hired to drive the herd from Nabachtoolik, western Alaska, to Kittigazuit, on the east side of the delta. He and his Inuit helpers travelled on foot over uncharted territory. The trek was expected to take eighteen months; it took five years.

Since 1972, the herd, which now numbers thirteen thousand animals, has been privately owned. Four permanent herders look after the reindeer, herding them along their seasonal migration pattern.

Because no additional grazing land is available, there must be an annual harvest of reindeer to control overpopulation. This harvest provides the owner with enough income to maintain a highly professional operation. It is one of the few locally owned, self-sustaining industries in the north using renewable resources.

For the last six years I have inspected the meat and by-products for both local consumption and export from the Northwest Territories.

Gordon Godkin, DVM, Tuktoyaktuk

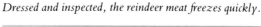

Dressed and inspected, the reindeer meat freezes quickly.

Here we are sitting on the edge of the world, a handful of people in a small community, and just a few miles from us these big oil companies settle down. They affect our lives so much. A lot of people work for them and bring home big pay cheques, but you miss a day or two and you are fired. Handling big money is not something you learn overnight, either. Some people make lots and some make none. It's a delicate situation, and we are in a state of transition. The companies make token efforts, but I think we are giving up more than we are getting. If we wanted to deal effectively with them, we would have to talk like them and think like them.

My generation is the first to go beyond grade nine. We went through the wringer, got in all the schooling. For ten years I was kept in school without ever going home to Sachs Harbour. When I finally got home, I was already a lost cause as a trapper—just a drifting school kid. My older brothers would set a thousand traps while I was looking after twenty-four. I finally became a forestry officer and worked in the south. If I don't want to be a labourer for one of the oil companies, there is nothing for me here.

Joseph Carpenter, Tuktoyaktuk

You think this is bad. You should hear the noise in the summertime: boats, ships, planes, choppers, trucks right around the clock.

Elisabeth Kimiksana, Tuktoyaktuk

Dome Petroleum's four drill ships moored at McKinley Bay

Central Arctic

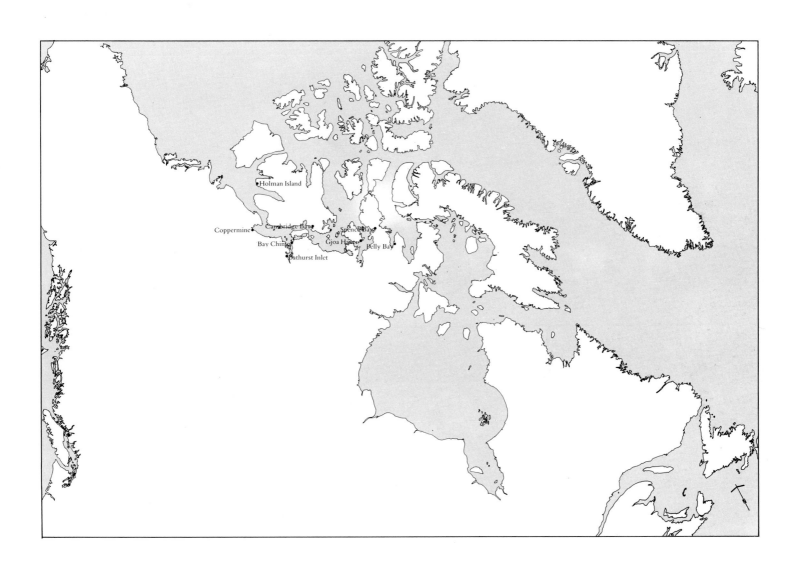

Inukshuk (man of stone) above Pelly Bay

Pelly Bay burial ground

When I was a child, we used to live all over the place—near Gjoa Haven, near Spence Bay. There was no white man and no priest. One winter my brother brought us a calendar that Father Henry had written down all by hand. There were black marks on it for Christmas, to tell us that there would be a feast. So we all walked from across the bay, because we had no dogs at the time. It was a long walk; we had to build an igloo for the night. When we got to Pelly Bay, we first went to visit with the Eskimos and then with Father Henry. He first shook hands and then he hugged me and then he rubbed noses with me. That same year I was baptized.

I was a teen-ager when they built that little stone church. It was just before that World War Two. Father Vandevelde did the woodwork inside, while Ataq and Oolik, the two brothers, together with Jack Itimangnak and Father Henry did the stonework.

Bernard Iqqugaqtuq, Pelly Bay

The little stone church and Father Henry's house

Barthelemy Nirlungayuk, lay catechist, during Sunday service

I went south twice: Edmonton, Saskatchewan. It's hot down there—I went in July—too hot to go outside. I was born in an igloo in January; maybe that's why I don't like it hot. At night you could not see outside. I am not used to dark nights in the summertime.

There are many people down south. They are like the seagulls, all talking and hollering at the same time. I could not understand them, got real homesick right away.

Guy Kringorn, Pelly Bay

Sunday dinner at the Kringorns' house

Just released from Yellowknife hospital, Jaqueline Kayasark, Pelly Bay, Celine Pauloosie, Spence Bay, and Rebecca Iquallaq, Gjoa Haven, waiting with their newborn babies for their flight home

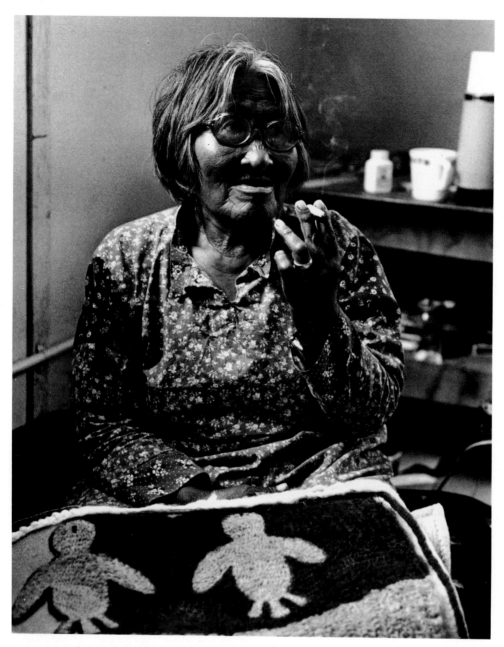

Helen Kringorn with tapestry

I never wanted to get married; I was very afraid of men. My family were begging me to get married to Jacob, but I did not want to marry. Most girls were afraid. We did not even want to see boys' faces. When they kept on begging me, I got married. I did not like it, but I had to stay with him. I am seventy-three years old and I really like him now.

Our children have to go hunting for us, now that we are old, and they do all the work. It is good to have children.

Helen Kringorn, Pelly Bay

White people were never around when we were kids; that's why we were scared of them. What if they would walk up to our camp and scold us and be unfriendly? After I got married I started seeing a lot of them. Since then I am not afraid any more. Now they even sleep in our house.

I was born in Natsilik, where Spence Bay is now. When I was young, before I started to know everything, my mother died. My grandfather taught me how to speak, how to make a bow and arrow, and how to shoot with it. He taught me how to hunt a seal with a harpoon, how to spear a fish, and how to hunt a caribou with bow and arrow. From that time on I was a hunter until I was old. When I was eight years old, I shot my first caribou with a gun. I am seventy-five now, and I get tired easily.

Jacob Kringorn, Pelly Bay

Jacob Kringorn makes a bow out of caribou antler and sinew.

John Kayasark and his cousin Columban Pujardgok at Tinitpajuk camp

I won my sleeping bag in a shooting competition two years ago—Eskimos against the Army. They came up to Pelly Bay, twenty-five of them, with a captain. The guy who won first prize for the army got a harpoon from our people. They were real nice guys from B.C. Three of them got frostbitten, the captain froze his toe, and the sergeant fell off the skidoo.

John Kayasark, Pelly Bay

Columban Pujardgok: I think I see fish . . . Let's hope there is fish.

We had some ice drift into the net last night and it ripped. We had to cut the
net, and lost half of it out there.

John Kayasark, Pelly Bay

We used to share everything. Even a bad hunter was all right as long as he was among other hunters. But now our customs have changed through the influence of missionaries, the RCMP, and all the different government agencies that come in here. Young people used to respect their elders more before there was a school here. That is what our old people say.

John Ningark, secretary manager of the hamlet office, Pelly Bay

Columban Pujardgok caches char to preserve it for the old people.

Drift ice

Tuvak (broken up ice) on Pelly Bay

The hamlet of Pelly Bay and part of the air strip

The project I work for is a government-sponsored survey to see whether it is possible to enlarge the commercial fishing industry in this part of the Central Arctic. Our team, two scientists and myself, is stationed here because Pelly Bay has a fish plant. I fly to all the outlying camps, including those around Gjoa Haven and Spence Bay, to collect the fish.

If the engine ices up, you have only one way to go, and that's down. You are not allowed to fly a single engine land plane over an open body of water unless you are within gliding distance of shore. Because of tundra tires, the plane can take off on fairly rough or soft surfaces. It is a STOL, a short takeoff and landing aircraft, just right for this type of work.

Ted Grant, pilot for the Department of
Economic Development and Tourism, Cambridge Bay

To get a barge into Pelly Bay is impossible. It would have to go all around Boothia Peninsula; it could get here, but not back, before the bay freezes up again. Everything has to be flown in, even the fuel. That means that our food is twice and three times as expensive as in other places in the North. We balance the prices somewhat by charging more for sweets, pop and junk food than for staple foods.

This co-op is run by the natives. We support ourselves through the sales at the store, through contracts—hauling goods from the air strip to the village—and through the money that comes in from the fish plant. We pay the fishermen by the pound, and the ladies who clean the fish, by the hour. Once the fish is frozen and packed we sell it to various consumers in Yellowknife.

Inuk Charlie, Co-op manager trainee, Pelly Bay

Barthelemy Nirlungayuk, supervisor of the co-op fish plant, talking to co-op employees

Children playing outside at night in Pelly Bay

Only the little old stone church was here when they built the school in 1963. Four years later the government put in the houses. All the families were still living in igloos.

An igloo is easier to keep up than a house. I don't remember ever being cold or uncomfortable in one. When it got too old and you had to patch it up every day, you just went ahead and built a new one.

We did not ask the government for houses; they offered them to us. After a few years they started raising the rent, and the people said, "We did not ask for the houses, and now that we have gotten used to them, the government is raising the rent on us." But there was nothing we could do.

Now, with seven kids, I don't think I'd ever want to live in an igloo again. The children have never known to live in one, and the space of a house is important. Even three bedrooms are not enough for us now. Everyone wants to go to bed at different times, particularly in summer when there is no school, when it is light all night long.

When you don't have a regular job, it is hard to raise a family, to buy all the clothes for school. Even with an income it is hard. We can't get away from the problems. I guess we are hooked on the white culture.

Celine Ningark, Pelly Bay

Sabina Anaittuq and her daughter Sheila polish caribou antler carvings.

The snow machines you send to us from the south constantly break down, and we have to order parts. How would you like it if you had to buy parts for the carvings we send to you?

Guy Kakkiarniut, Pelly Bay

When you look at the creating of settlements, you run into a lot of problems. Inuit coming from different areas were not used to living close together; they were used to spreading out in order to survive. But it is certain that the co-operative way is much in line with the spirit the people had before, when they were hunting and relying on each other's support. The co-operative is a modern application of the old Inuit way of life.

To start a co-operative you need a basic decency in the community. The Pelly Bay people were ready; they trusted each other and could co-operate.

Constructing a solid air strip on the land was a result of Pelly Bay's community spirit. It was built entirely by the people. Its purpose was to get the goods in cheaper and to secure fast transportation out for people who were seriously ill. People needed groceries, boats, guns, wood. Only by bringing in big aircraft could you reduce your cost per pound. Ships can't make it in and out in one season, and some years, you could not make an air strip on the ice.

With the growing market for fur, other needs kept coming up: bigger sleds, more dogs, which again meant more food for the dogs. After houses came to Pelly Bay in 1967, the needs of the community escalated even more and we decided to buy our own airplane, a DC 4. Later, that plane was taken over by the Co-op Federation.

Generally I would say government has been supportive of the co-operatives. But since government is subject to political implications—the administering of public funds, changing personnel—it makes for a lot of difficulties as well. The sooner the co-operatives can stand on their own feet, the better it will be.

Andrew Goussaert, chief executive officer of
Arctic Co-operative Ltd., Yellowknife

Construction crew of the new co-op building, Cambridge Bay

Flossie Oakoak, making turnovers at the Ikaluktutiax Bakery to fill an order for the co-op store in Gjoa Haven

The Inuit community of Cambridge Bay bears a social and cultural burden because of the very heavy outside influences: the DEW Line, the Hudson's Bay Company, the RCMP, the church, the Ministry of Transport, the government. While the agencies have a large part in creating this burden, they are also there to help solve it.

The territorial government has a hundred sixty-eight people on staff for the Central Arctic, serving maybe three thousand people. In addition, you have the staff of the federal government, RCMP, Northern Health and Welfare, and the Ministry of Transport. Out of our staff of sixty-nine people here in Cambridge Bay, twenty-eight are Inuit. Mind you, they are not in key positions yet. Ideally, my position should not be filled by a white man.

Larry Gilberg, assistant regional director, Central Arctic, Cambridge Bay

Even though we are all Inuit, every community and region is different from the other. To communicate these differences is what the Inukshuk Project is after. We have five ground stations in the Arctic.

Our video tape library is a record of the way of life of Inuit. People drop over sometimes and ask me to cover certain events, events that they care about and identify with.

This is an experimental project. When I heard ITC [Inuit Tapirisat of Canada] advertising the training program, I called right in. Really exciting, sort of being part of a space program, all of us Inuit communicating over a multimillion-dollar satellite. Bringing people together like this is a real privilege for me and gives me a good feeling.

David Tologanak, director of the Inukshuk Project, Cambridge Bay

David Tologanak

Charlie Evalik and Joey, his youngest boy

Section of the Cambridge Bay DEW Line complex

We have no control over the influences on this community. It is different from smaller places. We even have a hard time to teach our children the traditional skills. I am thinking of the movies, the game hall, and the small restaurant that the kids go to.

Even the language is going in this place. We are asking for school programs that would include the Inuit culture, but there is little impact, not in Yellowknife and not on the local level.

At the same time that we are pushing towards our own culture, we are trying to get the kids through grade twelve and maybe even more schooling—pushing them into the mainstream of white culture. That's where the conflict is.

The pressure is on not only in Cambridge Bay but also all over Inuit land. Explorations, and oil and mineral development, are pushing in on us. It is a temptation for Inuit to take jobs with those companies instead of just hunting and trapping and living off the land.

I too like to have my stereo and my TV—all the luxuries. I know that tomorrow I can go to the Hudson's Bay store and get my food there. It's much easier for my generation to take a job than to go hunting and fishing, and there are quite a few jobs available in this settlement.

Right now there is really no benefit coming to us from the northern industries other than employment. Once the land claims are settled it will be easier to accept development. More benefits will come our way and hopefully we will be in control over our land.

Charlie Evalik, Cambridge Bay

We are still watching and listening, the same as when the Distant Early Warning Line was constructed in 1954. Since then some sites were cut out due to more sophisticated equipment. There are DEW Line stations all the way from Alaska to Greenland. Here in Canada it is a joint venture between the American Air Force and the Canadian Armed Forces.

Walter Michalchuk, Canadian station supervisor,
Cambridge Bay DEW Line Site

Tank farm of Fred H. Ross and Associates, dealer for Imperial Oil. The tanks have a holding capacity of 735,000 gallons of heating oil, an ample year's supply for Cambridge Bay.

Ernie Boffa was a legendary bush pilot, one of a kind. We were the first men to mark the ice strips for the DEW Line sites in 1955. We had to land on the ice every fifty miles, where the sites were staked, to see whether it was safe for larger aircraft to land. This was in the middle of winter, of course. You could not tell whether you were landing on two inches of ice or on six feet; it all looked the same with the snow blowing over it. At that time you had no navigational instruments, no radio communication. You had to fly by the seat of your pants.

When they hired us, they didn't tell us what we were going to do. They didn't even put us on the payroll for the first week. Everything was hush hush.

Ole Hermanson, construction superintendent, Cambridge Bay

Oil drums being unloaded from an Electra at Coppermine airport

Garry Bristow distributes heating oil to the houses of Holman Island.

Manoeuvring the barges which bring yearly supplies and building material for Holman Island

The bay is full of ice. We've had ice problems for the last fifty miles. We are built for this, but if you get heavy winds and the ice starts moving, you want to get away from that stuff. I've been stuck in the ice to a position where I couldn't move any more. So you just sit there and wait. We start moving the barges in late July up to late September. You can't ever tell where it will freeze up first.

In the fall of 1974 we were breaking four to five inches of new ice and finally froze in at Herschel Island at Pauline Cove. They had to take us out by helicopter.

We can tow three barges at two thousand tons each. For Holman we used only two of them with goods for the Hudson's Bay, the co-op, the Housing Association, and the NCPC [Northern Canadian Power Commission].

There is bulk fuel on all the barges. Things come in containers now, no damage at all any more. Better service to the customers, less headaches for us.

Bob Magill, captain of the Kelly Hall, *Holman Island*

The children are paid well to unload containers for the Hudson's Bay store.

The biggest quantity of any single item we've brought in for the store is pop. It's got to be between twenty-five hundred and three thousand cases for a population of three hundred people. That's seventy-two thousand cans of pop. You never know; we might run out of it before next year's barge comes in.

Jim Klaassen, Hudson's Bay manager, Holman Island

Storing the year's supply of Pepsi

The empty barges leave four days after their arrival.

The government houses are supposed to be designed for the North. They change the design every year. They say they are trying to improve the heating quality. You don't know whom to make responsible if it doesn't work. Some architect from the south gets the contract, and the professional carpenters here have to follow the government blueprint. The local housing association decides where to place the houses—anywhere, in the swamps or on gravel pads. Some of them move and the wind gets at them, and the doors don't work and you have to fly in new ones. All the old matchboxes leak through the roofs. Even the new Hudson's Bay store is leaking.

I've been in the Central Arctic for fifty-two years, working for the Hudson's Bay Company. We started out just travelling along the coast to find a place to build a post. They couldn't tell us in Vancouver where to go; they didn't know. That was in 1928. We built a house and we built a store fifty miles east of where Coppermine is now. There was nobody within two hundred miles of us. The boat, and the mail, came only once a year. We had no heat in the store, didn't need it. We traded just once a year, at Easter time. The Eskimos stayed at the coast for only a month, then went inland. I trapped in the winter; there was nothing else to do. There was just the carpenter, the manager and I, and the carpenter soon left to help build Coppermine.

Later I worked for the Hudson's Bay all over the Central Arctic. Now I've been in Holman almost twenty years. I guess we'll be staying here.

Bill Joss, agent for Northwest Territorial Airways, Holman Island

Bill Joss and his son Stephen Holman Joss

Collin Dickie, assistant manager of the Hudson's Bay store, buying and grading sealskins

Roy Inuktalik working with whalebone

Alec Banksland

When I make my prints, I follow old stories from my dad and my mom. They both died long ago, but I remember.

This is what my father saw. Two old shaman liked to play together and outdo each other. One was carrying a seal oil lamp of stone. He stretched it out very long and then let it go back together again. The other man was watching that and then he went to a big log that was stuck deep into the ground. He made little noises and the log came out of the ground and laid on the land.

One shaman was talking about his death because it was coming close to him. He said he wanted to be put out on the beach when he died, because he did not want to be buried in the ground. So after he died, his family put him on the shore. Then all of a sudden all the walrus from the ocean came in big waves to that shore and pulled the body into the ocean. That man must have been one of the walrus; that's why they came to get him.

Just a few people come from animals. When I was small I knew a man who came from the polar bears. He had a low voice and was big. That man knew when he was a cub and his bear mother was bringing him to the land from the ocean. He remembered it. He saw these two big hills when his mother was taking him to the land, and he knew he was never going to leave them.

So the mother brought him to the people at night. For a while the cub could not remember anything. The next thing he knew was going into a woman's womb, and all the time he was in his mother's womb until he was born.

When he grew up, he was not afraid of anybody because he was from the polar bears. And he could just tear the meat out from the middle of the muktuk.

When I was small, I used to hear all about that man that I knew.

Alec Banksland, Holman Island

Kate Inuktalik and her family go seal hunting.

Connie Alanak skins a seal.

University Library
GOVERNORS STATE UNIVERISTY

Sealskins drying

Ice floats in August

Mark Emerak

Come springtime my dad still likes to go hunting. He just takes off with the skidoo. We are getting used to letting him go. He never goes too far. He still hunts caribou. Anyone can get them, even a child; they come right to the airport.

Nicholas Uluariuk, Holman Island

When I think back, there was nothing, just our people living on the land. There was bows and arrows, seal, fish and caribou. All the time while I was young, we never stayed in one place. We were looking for the caribou. All the time we were hunting caribou, for clothing, for meat, and for tents. And when the snow started coming, everybody moved to the ocean and put up their tents and waited for enough snow to make igloos. There was always one real big igloo in the middle with many holes to get in. Everybody helped to make that big igloo. There we would dance to the drums. We were happy at that time.

Now people look happy, maybe, but for different reasons. Sometimes it is liquor that makes them happy. They are not happy the way we were when we were young, when we all got together.

I was adopted. I never had my mother's milk, just seal gravy and fish gravy. They cooked it. We made fire with rocks. We made sparks and lit the cotton grass for the stone lamps and used the seal blubber for oil. We handled the cotton grass most carefully; it was the most important thing. We made a little bag from the caribou skins to store it. All the clothes were caribou skin. Summer and winter we wore caribou skin till all the fur fell out.

Now I am smoking and use a lighter. It's so easy. But often I think about how it was—about the rocks we used.

Agnes Nigiyok, Holman Island

Cotton grass (Eriophorum polystachion)

Holman Island cemetery at midnight

Now everything is going so fast, so wild—all the things from the white people. Our little ones all speak English. It's like we are drifting apart.

When I am with older people, we talk about the fast changes. It makes us feel sad. It can't be stopped; it's gone too far. I like my old oil stove, but when it breaks down I will only be able to get an electric one.

Elisabeth Banksland, Holman Island

Lichen and prickly saxifrage (Saxifraga tricuspidata)

Keewatin

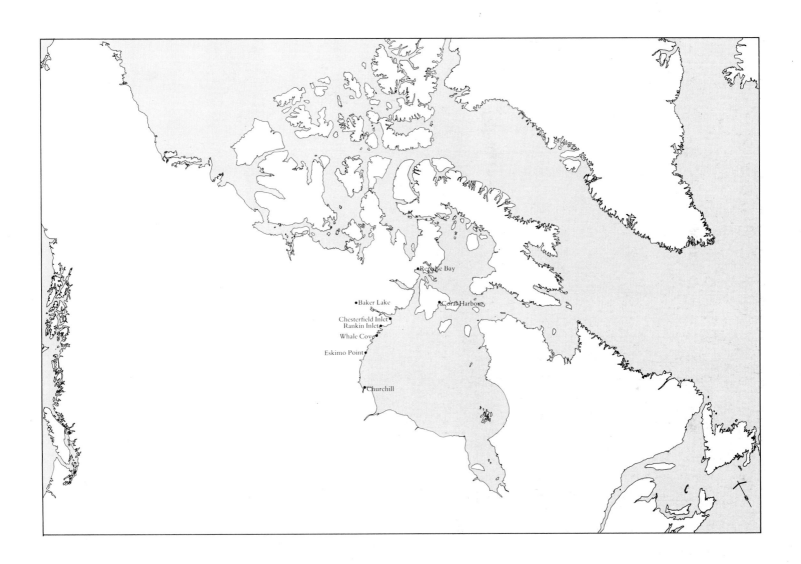

Repulse Bay

• Baker Lake

Coral Harbour

Chesterfield Inlet
Rankin Inlet

Whale Cove

Eskimo Point

Churchill

When Inuit were still strong, before kablunaat, they played games with rocks all the time.

Peter Suwaksiuk, Eskimo Point

Inuit made inukshuks all over the land. They did not have CBs and radios. If there was good fishing, they put up rocks to tell the next guy where to fish. If there were caribou, they made big inukshuks to hide behind. When the caribou came close, they shot them with bow and arrow.

Jimmy Muckpah, Eskimo Point

Inukshuk at Kaminak Lake

Caribou near Kaminuriak Lake

Jimmy Muckpah, minister of the Eskimo Point Anglican Church

The tent is fastened on either side to a sled to protect it from the fierce winds.

Hunters and trappers of Eskimo Point, like Peter Suwaksiuk, rent CB radios for long trips.

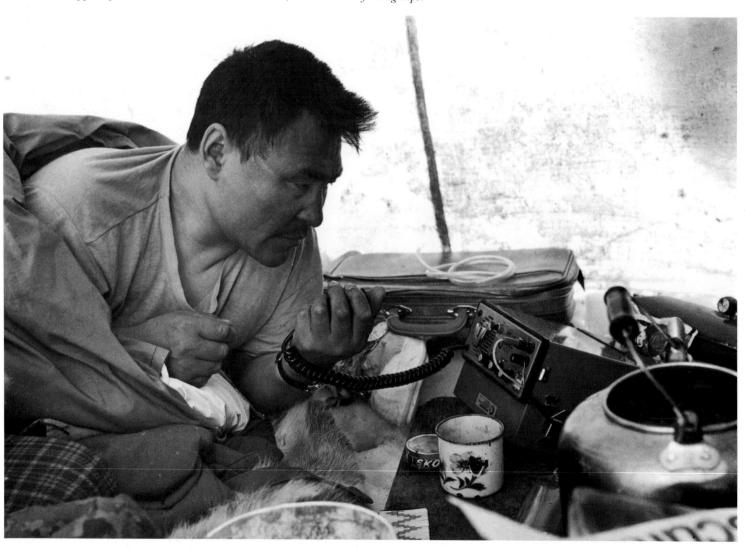

Joseph Aggark, Joshua Curley and Rosie Aggark visit Peter Suwaksiuk and Jimmy Muckpah near Maguse Lake.

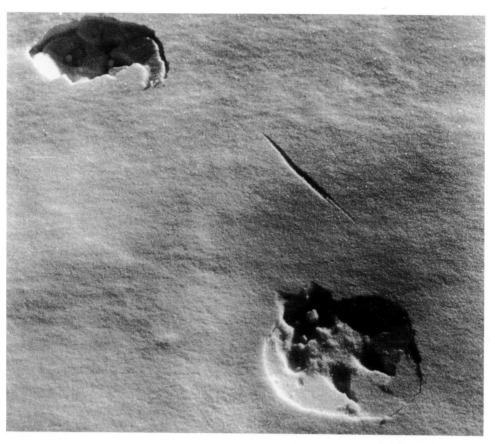

Wolf tracks

One day Kiviuk drifted in his kayak away from Eskimo Point. He drifted out towards the ice. When he reached it, he started walking and he walked and walked all the way to the other side of the Hudson Bay. There he found an old lady and her daughter. He stayed with them in their house and married the daughter, but he always left his kamiks and his mitts and some food at the shore.

One day Kiviuk went hunting. While he was away, the mother was taking the wax out of her daughter's ear with a long needle. Sticking the needle right through her ear, she killed her, because she was jealous of her. Then she skinned her daughter's head and put the skin over her own face.

When Kiviuk came back from hunting, the woman said, "Go down to the shore to your kayak." But Kiviuk said to her, "First take your kamiks off." When she took them off, he saw that it was the mother; her feet looked dark and old.

Kiviuk got ready to leave. When the old lady saw that, she told him that he would be seeing terrible things. She was a shaman.

Kiviuk went to the shore, took his kamiks, his mitts, his food and went off with his kayak across the water and the ice and the islands of Hudson Bay. Soon he saw two big bears fighting. He tried to get around them, but they were always in front of him. So he put his kayak on his head and went right through them.

Some time later he saw a big kettle full of boiling water. He tried to get around it, but it was always in front of him. So he climbed over it and got to the other side.

Next he saw two big mountains moving back and forth towards each other. When he could not get around them, he ran between them. His pants got caught and they ripped, but Kiviuk got through.

Then he saw the hind of a fat caribou. It was too big to get around it so he ate his way through it.

The last thing he saw was the bottom half of a woman's body. When he could not get around it, he fucked it and went through.

Finally Kiviuk arrived at the igloos of Eskimo Point. His parents had long thought that he was dead. When they heard that he was alive, they died on the spot. On that rock where they were sitting, you can still see the imprints of their seats and of their feet.

Peter Suwaksiuk, Eskimo Point

Wolf skin

Elisabeth Muckpah with her adopted daughter Samantha, cleaning a wolf skin. Wolf is the best fur for trimming parkas.

My first child died at birth. I had carried it for only seven months. At that time we were still living in tents. The second child died from pneumonia. There were no nurses at the time, no doctors. The RCMP in Pond Inlet had some pills, but we were living too far from them. One of my babies got bitten so badly by the dogs that it was dead by the time we reached the RCMP by dog team. Another baby died from a bad stomach ache. Not long ago, my grandson had the same stomach ache. We sent him to the hospital in Winnipeg and they helped him. It is so different today; we get quick help from the nursing station whenever we need it.

The doctors say I have no sickness, but I always feel sick when I think about the past and how my babies died.

Elisabeth Muckpah, Eskimo Point

The cemetery at Repulse Bay

Eric Anoee

A sudden change of temperature at the end of May transforms Eskimo Point.

Very few people in Eskimo Point are native to this area. They moved here from inland, and from Coral Harbour, north of here. My mother was from inland, my father from the coast near Eskimo Point. There was of course no settlement here at that time. People were out on the land hunting caribou in the summer and fall, and they stayed for the winter near the places where their meat was cached and where there was good fishing in the lakes. They also trapped white fox. Came springtime, they moved to the coast to hunt for seal and to trade fur and seal blubber in Churchill.

Most of the white fox is gone now. There was too much trapping in the thirties when Baker Lake and Chesterfield Inlet opened trading posts closer than Churchill. I remember going to Churchill by boat. There were old Indian people there talking Inuktitut.

This is the most southern Inuit community on our side of Hudson Bay. The Anglican mission and the Roman Catholic mission were already here in 1926. Then the RCMP came in. But it was not until 1961 and 1962 that the first one-room houses were built. It was the nickel mine in Rankin Inlet that made people move to the coast for employment. The mine closed after five years, but the people stayed. Today less than half of the Inuit in Eskimo Point are hunters. The caribou are far away most of the year, and gas for skidoos is too expensive. There is no way we can move back to the land. We would not be able to afford clothing, and there would not be a nursing station. But people here live much in the old ways.

As a member of our education society, I have been out recruiting teachers. It is rare to find a teacher who speaks Inuktitut. Some of them stay long enough to learn, but many leave after one or two years. Since hardly any of our parents speak English, there is very little communication between them and the teachers. This sometimes creates problems.

My big concern is with the spending of money. Nobody here makes very much, yet the children spend it on sweets and pop, asking again and again for more. The parents have a hard time saying no because refusing food is not part of their tradition.

Eric Anoee, Justice of the Peace, Eskimo Point

For the last three years I have been chief land claims negotiator for ITC, although we didn't start negotiations until November of 1980. Two years ago, when our national organization, Inuit Tapirisat of Canada, was not satisfied with the progress made by the Land Claims Commission, they abolished the commission and took over control. They said that they would possibly have an agreement within six months. Unfortunately or fortunately this was not realized. It was far more difficult than they anticipated. They found out that we have a huge land to deal with, twenty-seven communities, seventeen thousand people. Things fell apart. The federal election came along, the Conservatives got in. Before they had a chance to deal with the policy, a new government came back again. Finally, last year, Munro started to get the ball rolling.

We drafted the Nunavut proposal, a political development paper for the creation of a separate territory within the Northwest Territories. Realizing that land claims will not leave us with much land, we feel that our Nunavut government would be able to exercise a certain amount of political control. Since territories don't control land or resources, we hope at least to be able to assert more political pressure than the Northwest Territories government does.

On the actual land claims scene, we have identified and consolidated a number of objectives. Basically we are going for harvesting rights, land and money, with subdivisions for education, communication and so on.

We like to avoid division, the breaking away of communities. That is one of the reasons we are taking such a long time in spite of the impatience of many Inuit. We have been trying to prepare ourselves, and prepare materials, to inform the people as much as we can, so they know roughly what they will be getting into. We want to avoid a repetition of the situation in Quebec where the land claims agreement was rushed, and where three communities said they didn't know what they were giving away.

Thomas Suluk, chief negotiator for land claims for
Inuit Tapirisat of Canada, Eskimo Point

Canadian Imperial Bank, Rankin Inlet

Produce at the Hudson's Bay store

The "hangout" at the Rankin Inlet Lodge

Hudson's Bay Company store, Rankin Inlet

Spring games at Baker Lake: a three-mile race for boys

A dog race, part of the spring games at Baker Lake

Square dance at the community hall

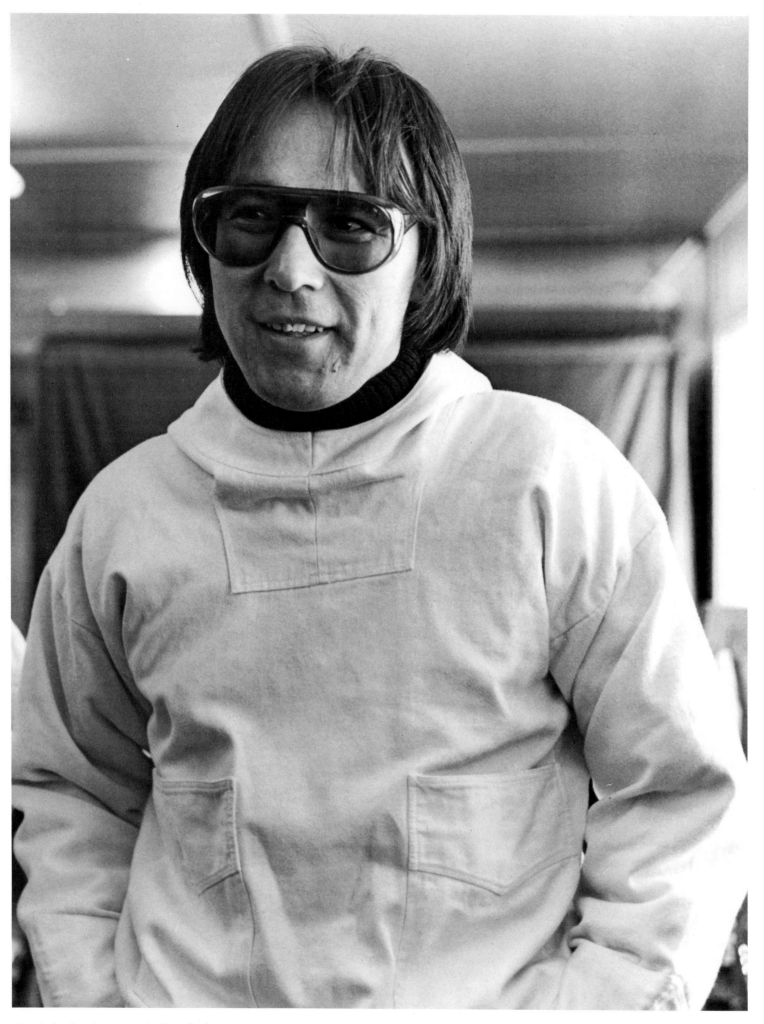

Jens Lyberth, who grew up in Greenland

We are trying to develop leadership and self-confidence, to enable Inuit to stand on their own, to stand in front of meetings, public hearings, negotiations without sweating or shaking, without blushing or stuttering. This is essential for the future of the North. So far we don't have many such people.

There are different kinds of development in Canada's North: industrial, governmental and political development. Eager and well-meaning people in those groups have forgotten the local people whose lives are subject to their decisions.

When industry invests a billion and a half dollars in the North, it means that they are going to stay for quite some time. There is nothing wrong with that, but the local people are not involved in that process. The only practical benefits are some wages.

The general income in the North has come through the welfare office, child care assistance program, unemployment insurance and pensions. Some money has come from arts and crafts, and from the little employment there is, but the control is still in the hands of the government.

In a rushed effort to get to the point of land claims settlement, which will permit decentralized control, the leadership of the political development has not had the time or manpower to assist the people in the settlements and hamlets, though everyone is full of good intentions.

Look, for example, at Baker Lake. It has about thirty-five local groups with their own boards of directors of nine members each, and there are less than a thousand people here. Again, everything is well intended.

It is my job to help people to think ahead, beyond land claims, governmental and industrial development. Where do they want to be ten years from now?

I helped to develop the idea of the Circumpolar Conference for Inuit from Alaska, Canada and Greenland. It was designed to get the political leadership to see beyond their own regions, beyond their national boundaries. That was difficult five, six years ago. But the concept of mankind exists in the Inuit language. Linguistically, Inuit means mankind, not people.

One hundred and thirty thousand Inuit are living on three million square miles of land, the richest part of the world—the only undivided social, cultural and linguistic group in such a large territory. So they have something going for themselves.

Jens Lyberth, responsible for Inuit Affairs for the Bank of Nova Scotia, Ottawa, conducting an ITC Leadership Workshop in Baker Lake

I am an ordained minister, but years ago I resigned from the Anglican Church. My idea was to tell my people: You can do it, you don't have to wait for kablunaat to do your services, you can do it yourselves; you can bring the good news. If you can run co-ops, you can run the churches too. We call our church Christian Arctic Fellowship.

To be truthful, my name should be Tagunrnaaq Armand, because I was Tagunrnaaq first and baptized later. Everybody is given an Inuit name by their father and mother. Before she gives birth, the mother may dream of a person, a name, and we believe that he is coming through us, so we give him that name.

I have my grandmother's name, my mother's mother; she was Tagunrnaaq. Louis Tapatai marries my mother. He calls Tagunrnaaq Mother-in-law. So here I am, also called Tagunrnaaq. Naturally my father calls me Mother-in-law and I call him Son-in-law, because my mother is my daughter, daughter of Tagunrnaaq, and she calls me Mother.

This custom is dying out. For instance, I talk to the RCMP and he asks, who is Louis Tapatai to you? If I say, he is my son-in-law, how could he understand? I have to say, he is my father. How could anybody understand if we used this old custom? It is out of date.

Armand Tagunrnaaq, minister, artist, and CBC reporter, Baker Lake

After many years, the caribou have returned to the area and the community has a surplus of meat.

I am going to the fish lake
I make the hole in the ice
and I jig for fish
āia āia ia ia ia aiā
There is no fish
there are no bites
there is nothing
āia āia . . .
I want to move on
down to the island
to hunt for caribou.
āia āia . . .
I see a caribou
and I get it
āia āia . . .
In the afternoon I see a polar bear
and I get it too
āia āia . . .
Now I am very happy in my body
in my caribou parka
Now I have lots of food
āia āia ia ia ia aiā

Louis Tapatai, Baker Lake
[Song by his uncle Iqaluk from Repulse Bay]

High winds in the beginning of May at Baker Lake

Matthew Innakatsik with one of his grandchildren

We are Back River people, different from the Baker Lake people and the ones from the coast. A long time ago we were very poor. Many people were starving and died. If they didn't hunt well or work well, they starved to death. You had to walk all day, walk after the caribou, walk after the birds, after the bear. You walked all day and never stopped. After you caught food, at night you ate. Yes, once a day you ate. Today's children don't know that; they eat all the time.

To make a fire, we had a stick and we twisted it with a string. The string was made of cut-up caribou skin and that is also what we used for fishing. We had caribou antler knives to make igloos, caribou antler harpoons to catch seal, bow and arrows, shovels, all from caribou antler. I don't know how old I was when I got my first gun, but I was already a man.

From Back River we walked to Gjoa Haven for seal. And we walked to Baker Lake to pick up tea, sugar, cigarettes, matches, bullets—only the things we really needed. We never picked up clothes. We wore caribou skins and kamiks. When the kamiks got holes, we put on another pair. I needed five to six pairs to walk to Baker Lake and back. Then I gave them to her and she fixed them again.

I go only by skidoo now, so my kamiks don't have any holes.

Matthew Innakatsik, Baker Lake

Long time ago people don't have any meetings—just talk to him and to him and to him. Now there is all kinds of meetings, people travelling all over by plane. It's all different now.

Up north people don't fight. First war, I am just a boy. Second war, I work for RCMP, I take them around by dog team. Now I am old, I listen to the news. Always bad news, always fight, troubles all over the world. I don't know why. I go to Eskimo Point, Rankin, Igloolik; we never fight. I talk with them over the CB, always happy, no fight. I walk down the road, people come my way; they stop, they talk. In the city nobody say hello. Maybe there is too many of them.

Louis Tapatai, Baker Lake

Toona Iqulik and his daughter Camilla, using the radio telephone at Louis Tapatai's house

Luke Anguhadluq and Bogus Zdyb, artistic director at the Sanavik Co-operative

In the past the inventiveness for making tools for survival came out of the igloo. This imaginative strength has found its new form in the art and still comes out of the home. The potential of the art in Baker Lake is unlimited. The way it is growing reminds me of a snake shedding its skin, leaving the old behind, emerging.

Bogus Zdyb, artistic director of the Sanavik Co-operative, Baker Lake

Rita Oosuak at Inuit Pitqosii, the Baker Lake craft shop, making an ulu

Sharpening the ulu

One lady never wants to get married, so her father asks her to marry a dog and she does. When she gets children, they are puppies, so she puts them into the bottom of her boots and lets them float away, out into the sea. The ones she tells: "You will be white people, kablunaat, and you will make things, big things, smart, intelligent." The others she tells: "You will be Indians, you will hunt with bow and arrow." And they disappear.

That is why kablunaat have so much hair and are coloured like dogs. We call ourselves Inuit, human beings, not animals. But we call you Inuit anyway when we see you in distance.

Armand Tagunrnaaq, Baker Lake

Sculpture by Johnny Iqulik

Phillippa Iksiraq, rubbing a stone print at the Sanavik Co-operative

Wall hanging by Ruth Tulurealik at the Miqsuqvik Sewing Centre, Baker Lake

Northern Quebec

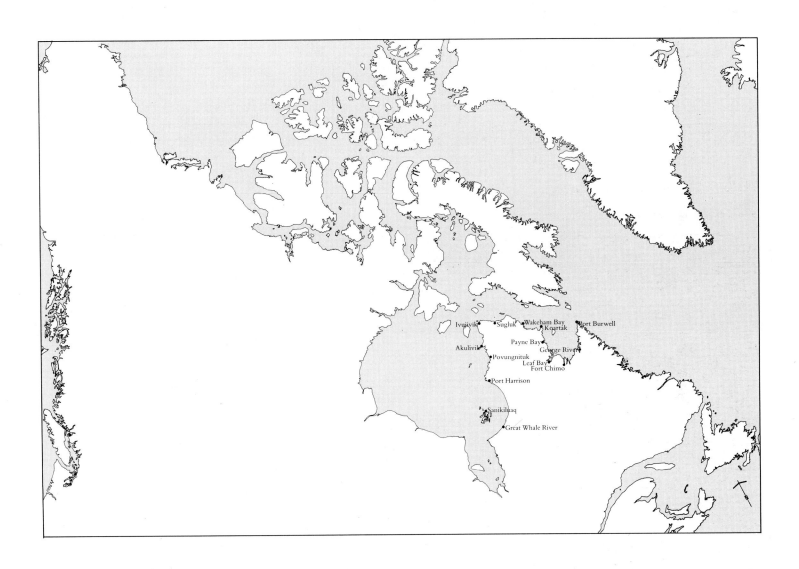

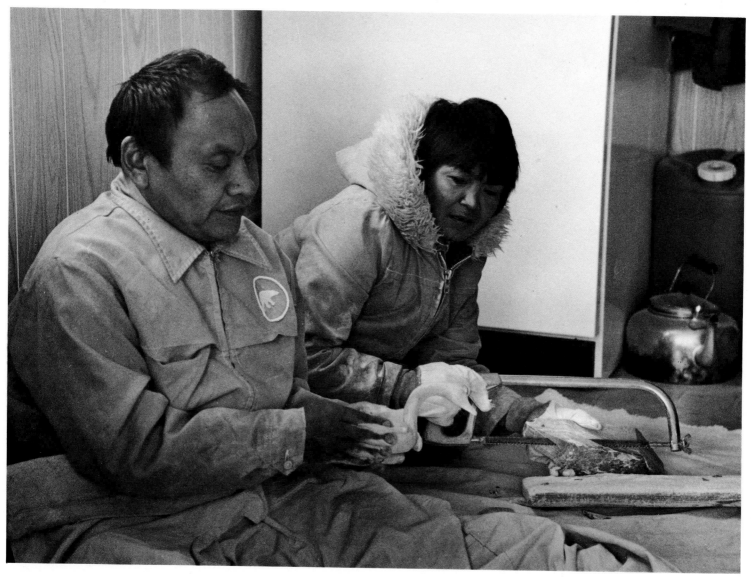

Charlie and Bessie Crow, Sanikiluaq

One winter several centuries ago, a heavy rain came down. Afterwards the islands froze over and all the caribou starved to death. This is what our elders told us. Even now, when you dig in the ground, you can sometimes find antlers. The territorial government brought sixty reindeer from Tuktoyaktuk in a big plane. That herd has spread to different parts of the islands, but the reindeer don't seem to multiply as fast as we had hoped. We watch them and take counts. Nobody is hunting them yet.

The Belcher Islands belong to the Northwest Territories even though most of the people here are related to Inuit from Quebec. My father's people came from there—Richmond Gulf. I guess Crow is an Indian name. Many Inuit names were spelled wrong by the RCMP who used to come over here in the early thirties. They didn't know our language and spelled the names the way they heard them. When our children began to go to school, they found out that the majority of their names were spelled wrong. Now this is slowly being corrected. We care, because most of our names have meanings, which are often taken from nature.

From the first week in July to the middle of August we camp on Tuqajaq Island, twenty-five miles east of here. Bessie, my brother and I go together to mine our soapstone there. We take all the tools along in the boat—shovel, axe, wedge, you name it. There are two mines. One has this light stone, the other has the dark one; that's the harder one to work with. Bessie and I do all our work together because I am blind.

Charlie Crow, Sanikiluaq (Belcher Islands)

Carvings by Bessie Crow

The frozen bay at Povungnituk becomes a speedway for snowmobiles.

Before the James Bay Agreement came into effect, there was always happiness among the people. They did not worry about anything but their own lives.

The agreement says that the northern Quebec Inuit and the James Bay Cree give up their rights to the land in exchange for Category I lands [reserves] for money, hospitals, schools and other services.

We looked into the final agreement. We studied it carefully and then we disagreed with it. We did not sign it; neither did Ivujivik and half the community of Sugluk. We did not want to give up our land nor did we want the money.

The James Bay Agreement went into effect just the same. One hundred and fifty million was paid for the land and seventy-five million for future development in northern Quebec, to be shared between Crees and Inuit according to population numbers. That means our future is already signed away. If the Inuit of the Northwest Territories sign a similar agreement, none of us Inuit will have a future.

We know that Inuit were here long before white people came to Canada. It looks like the white government just wants to step on us. If we lose our land, we will lose our culture; we will have no choice but to follow the white people's ways. To protect ourselves, we have hired a lawyer and are preparing for court action. We will fight not only for the Povungnituk people but also for all who signed and didn't sign the James Bay Agreement. We are financing the lawyer with the help of the local co-op and with local taxes. Some of the other communities who didn't know what they were signing, even some from the Northwest Territories, are helping us out of their pocket. We are neither getting nor wanting a cent from the government.

We don't really know the white man's way. Even if we work with him, we can't catch up with him. Instead of trying to work his way, we prefer to work our own way, using our culture and our language.

Our goal is to have our own government for all of northern Quebec. If we had a chair in parliament and were able to make our own laws, we would be satisfied.

Tamusi Qumak, Povungnituk
[Translated by Aisara Kenuajuak, president of the Community Council]

Povungnituk houses

Language program at the Povungnituk school

Alice Alushuak's native studies class, playing a game with syllabic symbols

Syllabic symbols

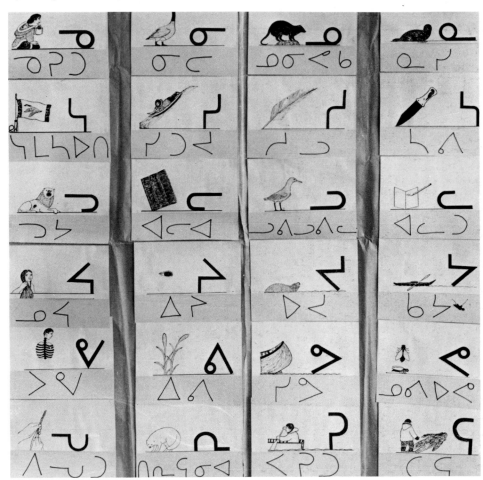

Alice Alashuak and Mary Sivuarapik, doing the katajak (a traditional way of singing from the throat)

Over twenty years ago, when the first school came into Povungnituk, the government said: Your children will have to go to school or you will not get your family allowance. If we educate your children they will be able to earn a lot of money. So the parents gave their children to the government school and stopped worrying about them growing up.

That is when we lost our will to survive as Inuit. Inuit used to trust anybody because they trusted each other completely. Trusting the government was a mistake. Now the parents are finding out what went wrong and they are starting again to be concerned about their children. They want them to grow up to be good adults, willing to work, but it is hard to make a fresh start under the existing conditions.

Annie Uqaituk, president of the Parents Committee, Povungnituk

Mary Sivuarapik, playing country fiddle at a party

We closed our school from 1979 to 1980; we refused to be under the Kativik school board, which had come to life as a result of the James Bay Agreement. Kativik believes they are doing the right thing by training and hiring Inuit teachers, but these teachers receive the same training as white teachers and we see them just as translators of a foreign culture and education. Rather than going back to the Kativik school board, we asked the minister of education to reopen our school.

That does not mean that our children are learning the things that concern their lives in the North. We teach them Inuktitut and some traditional crafts and culture, but other than that they just learn reading and writing and math, nothing more useful. The seventeen white teachers, who for the most part speak French, come from the south and bring us a southern education and all the materials that go with it.

Our school goes to grade ten. Maybe three or four students out of two hundred have graduated from high school. None of the others want to leave Povungnituk, not even for the two years it takes them to finish up.

There are some jobs here to be taken over, but it is hard to find qualified young people. The school so far does not prepare them for the kind of work that is available. We have not yet created the program we need. We are still working on it. It is very difficult, but we won't give up.

Dora Sallualuk, president of the Education Committee, Povungnituk

School children eat lunch at home.

Lunch for a nursing mother

Bewildered by the landing of an airplane, Bobby Novalinga's dogs get tangled in the atsuna (sealskin rope)

Bobby Novalinga, jigging for cod through an aurak (crack in the sea ice) for dog food

Timothy and Minnie Assapak with their uqutaq (wind shelter), built for ice fishing

Timothy Assapak, lake fishing for char and whitefish

The co-op store in Povungnituk

Our forefathers supported each other. That was their way to survive. The co-operative movement, even though it was first introduced to us by some southerners, is our only chance to keep our forefathers' culture alive.

I can say that because I have been working with the co-op from the beginning. Before we started it, people were highly dependent on the Hudson's Bay store or on individual hunters who brought the meat in. Without the co-op it would be worse today and more people would not have work and be dependent on welfare. We hire people who have not had a southern education and who don't speak English, like the carvers, printers and ladies in the sewing shop. I, for example, can't speak English. When I started, I had never dealt with figures. Now I am dealing with figures in the millions. I know how to manage our co-op and how to keep it out of financial trouble.

I am afraid that the co-operatives will be pushed aside by the business ventures that have come into northern Quebec since the James Bay Agreement. The Makivik Corporation in Fort Chimo, which is in charge of investing the land claims money, works in a very different way than we do. They only hire people with education.

We do not accept any money from Makivik even though we sometimes run short of funds. It is important to us to stay in control. We would rather have it this way. The marketing of carvings needs to be controlled by the co-op federations.

The life of any co-op depends on its members. Here, it has the support of the total population.

Tamusi Tulugak, general manager of the Povungnituk Co-operative
[Translated by his son Harry Tulugak, store manager]

161

Interior of the co-op store

Minnie Assapak, making kamiks

Jusi Sivuarapik at the print shop

This print shop is a happy place; we run it ourselves. We produce three kinds of prints: silk screen, stencil and stone prints. The artists bring in the cut soapstone plate; for silk screen and stencil prints they supply us with drawings. We decide what colours to use. Our print editions are small, no more than fifty. In one day a printer may put out one, two or three prints. Most of the time is taken up by preparatory work. We put out thirty new prints last year.

Jusi Sivuarapik, manager and printer, Povungnituk Print Shop

Prints drying

Timarq, wrapping carvings at the co-op store in Sugluk for shipment to Montreal

I would rather stay home and carve than go out to work. I like to make carvings of people that go hunting, and of animals. We were still living in igloos and tents when I learned to carve—maybe thirty years ago.

I have seen Japanese and Chinese carvings. They look a little bit like ours, but they are made from different material, like my tea cup. Have you been in Greece? They make fine carvings too.

When I was in Montreal I saw white people carving soapstone like we do. I don't like that. I also saw copies of Inuit carvings in the stores. That is bad. I would not think of copying white people's carvings.

Sometimes I stop carving because I have a pain in my lungs from the dust. Now one lung is no good.

Levi Qumaluk, Povungnituk

Timothy Assapak, carving beside his house

Levi Qumaluk does the rough carving of the soapstone in a tent next to his house.

Tivi Ilisituk, Sugluk, carves far enough away from his home not to be disturbed.

The Sugluk ice strip is the connecting point for Austin Airways, which serves the west coast of northern Quebec, and Air Inuit, which serves the Ungava Bay area.

Asbestos Hill. In 1979 the Asbestos Corporation Ltd. extracted over seven million tons of rock from this mine. Western Europe is the corporation's biggest client.

Kakinik Naluiyuk with his sons Charlie and Markusie

The Makivik Corporation was set up to handle the land claims money through investment, to create as much employment and economic development as possible for the Inuit of northern Quebec. The James Bay Agreement looked good in the beginning, and we supported it, but it turned out not to meet our needs. We were told by the white experts that our investments would make money in the first year and more every year after. Everybody was happy. But nothing worked. Without the right people—real experts—we are losing both money and credibility. Air Inuit is not making it; the fishing company is not making it; the construction company is not making it. We have already lost over twenty million dollars and we don't have many jobs for the people, which was our main objective.

Northern Quebec has a real problem: people don't know how to run their own affairs. White people don't know how an Inuk thinks; I don't know how a white man thinks. I can see what he does, but I don't know what he thinks. So I can't support his ways. We need people to find out just how the white man thinks.

We are living in two cultures. We know our own, but we don't understand what makes the television run, or the stove, or how to repair them—all the things from the south that we have and want. We are trapped without realizing how it happened.

Kakinik Naluiyuk, former vice-president of the
Makivik Corporation, Sugluk

Dr. André Laurin comes to Sugluk twice a year and stays for three weeks. He brings with him 800 pounds of dental equipment, including a dental chair.

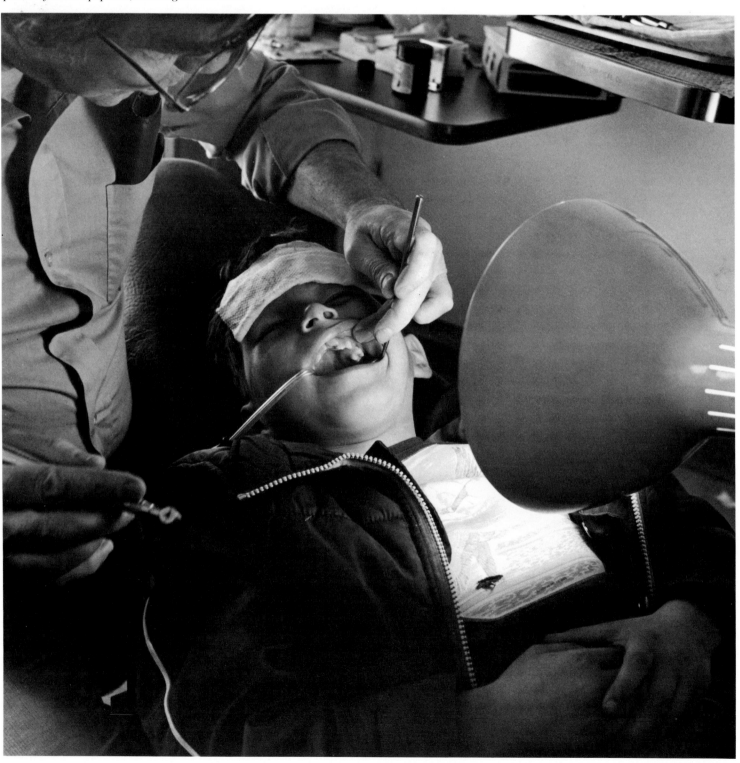

Half the community of George River comes out for the fish race at the week-long Easter games.

The tea race: whose pot will boil first?

The tea pots have been brought in, and people are busy preparing the communal Easter dinner.

The weather changes fast around here. Before you know it, it starts blowing snow. That is one of the reasons people travel together, maybe three or four skidoos at a time. If a man goes by himself, he tells his family where he is going to hunt, but even then it is hard to find a guy who is lost. We are used to looking out for each other.

We took some kids out camping. When we told them to get firewood, they cut down live trees instead of dead ones. They did not understand the word for dry wood. Many words are used out on the land that the children don't ever hear in the community, for example, words for different parts of a river or a lake. With the changing life style our language has become very poor.

Some of our children are learning French in school; others learn English. Maybe that is good. If they want to talk to each other, they will have to continue speaking Inuktitut.

Peter Morgan, George River

Joshua Annanack and Minnie Morgan at Short Lake, near the Labrador border

Tent at night

Spruce branches provide insulation and a wonderful scent

Mary and Joshua Annanack and Minnie Morgan

Joshua Annanack, setting net for char fishing under the ice. Earlier in the season, a rope was fed through holes in the ice and fastened at both ends to poles; now the net can easily be set and pulled out again.

The story I am about to tell you happened in 1925, but to me it is like yesterday.

At that time we were living across Ungava Bay. One day close to breakup time, many hunters were going out for seal. They were all out on the ice when my grandfather Annanack, my uncle Tommy, and my little brother Josephie Amak Annanack floated away on the ice. All they had with them were their dogs and their qamutik [sled].

The wind was blowing from the south; they could not get back anymore, so they started to walk on the ice. Every day they walked, looking for thicker, safer ice. Some days it was warm, some days cold. They became very thirsty. (You can't eat snow; it makes you even more thirsty.) Annanack shot a walrus one day on top of the ice. He opened it up and cleaned it out. Then he put snow into it and it melted fast because the walrus was still warm. That day they drank lots of water.

They took pieces of the walrus meat and put it on the qamutik, and pieces from the walrus skin to sleep on. At night they pulled up big blocks of ice from the ocean and put them together for shelter; or if they had enough snow they built an igloo. Every night my little brother slept inside Annanack's parka, getting warm from his body. During the daytime they kept on walking.

Finally the wind changed and they got close to a small island that is called Paungaqtilik, not too far from Payne Bay. The ice was very thin, and they all kept running fast for fear that it would break under their feet. They barely made it to the island when all the ice disappeared.

One day a man came so close to the island with his kayak that they could even see him smoking his pipe. Annanack made the dogs bark loud, but he never listened to the dogs. When that man came home, his wife told him she had heard dogs yelling on the island, but the man said, "You didn't hear anything but yourself."

Annanack made a flag by putting his parka on the harpoon, but nobody saw it.

For nearly two weeks they waited. They had hardly any food when a big wind came from the north and brought ice all around the island. Annanack and Tommy and Josephie walked back to the land. They had been gone for more than a month.

My little brother was riding on the qamutik when they arrived at their home. He was so happy he just ran into the igloo in his little caribou parka. Everybody had thought he was dead. Annanack's wife just started yelling and crying.

My grandfather Annanack was a good man, always trying to help others. He knew the weather like nobody else did. When they came home that time I thought, after that they are not going to die no more. But of my family I am the only one alive now. I am seventy-one years old.

Lizzie Annanack, George River

Lizzie Annanack

Peter Morgan and Joshua Annanack, fixing a snowmobile motor

It looks like everything is breaking down today. First one skidoo, then another skidoo. Now Joshua saw some ptarmigan and could not shoot them: the rifle was frozen. If there is nothing much you can do, you can always laugh.

People before us were much stronger than we are and they could run much faster. They lived on ptarmigan, caribou, fish, seal—all the wild food. They could even smell the caribou from far away. We can't do that any more. We are polluting ourselves with all these junks around.

Peter Morgan, George River

Peter Morgan with his son Matthew

The Morgans' dog, bringing her newborn puppies into the warmth of the house

Matthew Morgan and his puppy

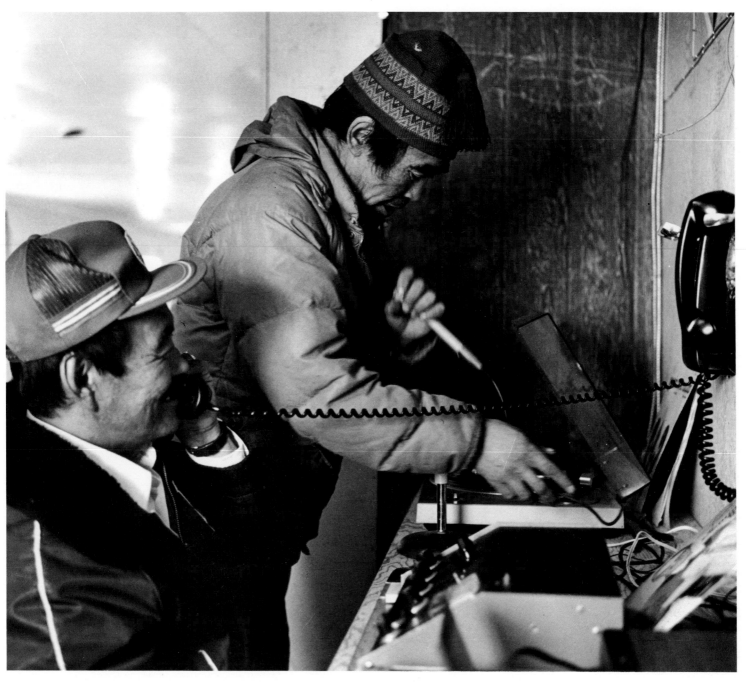

Willie Etok and Noah Annanack at the local FM station, George River

We had the first co-op in the north. Got it the year I was born: 1959.

This is the co-op way. If I need anything—caribou, fish, even sea otter skins—I just ask for it. I call the radio announcer, tell him what I want, and give him my phone number. Whoever has that thing will call back right away. No need to pay for it.

Minnie Morgan, George River

George River in April

Willie Emudluk in front of his store

We did not know what a co-op was when we had our first meeting with Don Snowden and John Evans in Frobisher Bay in 1957. We met for only two hours. They told us how the Indians had put all their carvings together in a big box and when they had enough, began to sell them.

Next year Don Snowden came, as promised, to old George River where I was the manager of the Hudson's Bay store. George Kumiak, who was a good translator, was with him. I guided the plane to the Korok River where most of the people were living at that time. In a meeting at Sammie Annanack's place they talked about the co-op—about logging, fishing, sewing, carving soapstone—and they promised us a small sawmill.

The people spent all spring until breakup time getting logs. At the same time, they built a small boat, big enough to bring the logs down the river. Since nothing is impossible for the government, they gave us an outboard motor for that boat.

A white guy was working with the logging group—a good teacher and a good man to work with. But there was one thing we can't forget: he had a lot of food—flour and sugar—which he would not share. He said it was his, and that he had worked for it and paid for it himself. He still had most of it left when they all came down the river with the logs.

The same guy told us that it was too hard to take the logs around the bay from the George River to the Korok River, where the town was supposed to be developed. That is why we are here today.

We earned money with the logs and started to freeze fish in a small plant at the mouth of the river. A year later we were able to buy plywood and nails to build houses. All the two by fours and the two by sixes were produced right here.

After two years the government stopped the logging and the fishing. Not enough big trees and a declining fish population. But the people still got money from carving, welfare, family allowance, and construction. Since we had not enough people to support two stores, the Hudson's Bay moved away and I became co-op manager. We used their old building to make a tourist camp.

After fifteen years the population had grown enough that I was able to start my own little store. But we are grateful the co-op came in here. It came at a time when the government planned to relocate the people from this area, scattering them in different directions—Baffin, Labrador, Chimo.

Willie Emudluk, George River

The Hudson's Bay store in Port Burwell don't make enough money. The company close her up in 1924. Many Inuit leave for Labrador at that time. We stay. The closest store is in Old George River. We go trading by dog team. Too far. Nineteen sixty we get co-op store. Life is good then. Port Burwell belongs to Northwest Territories. Better than Quebec government. More money.

Lots of animals in Port Burwell. Seal, fish, big halibut, polar bear, caribou, killer whale, white whale, ducks, geese, ptarmigan—lots of good food.

Five years ago they tell us to leave. Too much trouble for ships coming in. They take the nurse away to Frobisher Bay. People get sick, no nurse. That's no good. So all the people leave for Quebec—Wakeham Bay, Koartak, George River.

We want to go back. Maybe 1983, '84 we'll all go back. Yes, all the Inuit will go back to Port Burwell.

Noah Annatok, George River

Labrador

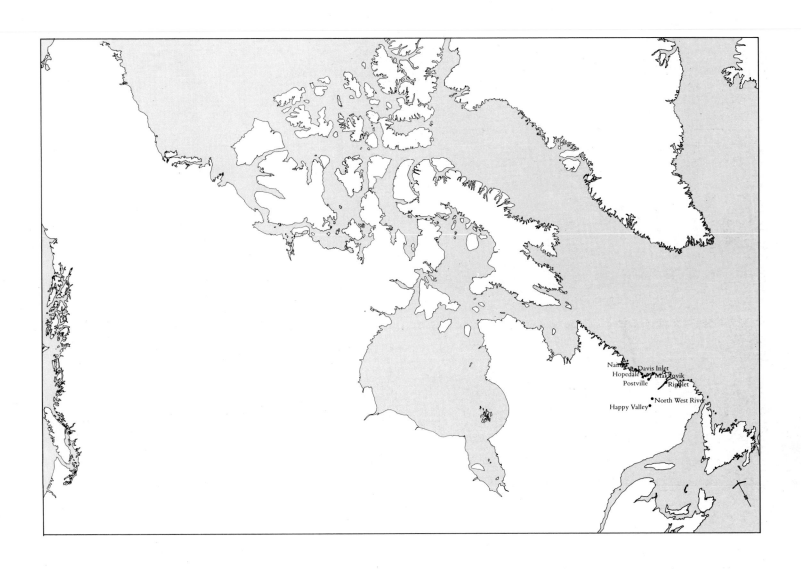

Nain • Davis Inlet
Hopedale • Makkovik
Postville • Rigolet
North West River •
Happy Valley •

The old Moravian mission in Hopedale

Kitora Boase has many visitors

There were many people in Okak when I grew up; lots of them and many boats. I went to the Moravian school when I was six, got out when I was thirteen. That is the way it was for everybody. After the Spanish flu it was not good in Okak any more. Only sixty people were left. In 1920, all the children and young people without parents came down to Nain, Hopedale, Makkovik.

The Germans are gone now. We have no more missionary in Hopedale. The last one went home to Denmark.

Kitora Boase, Hopedale

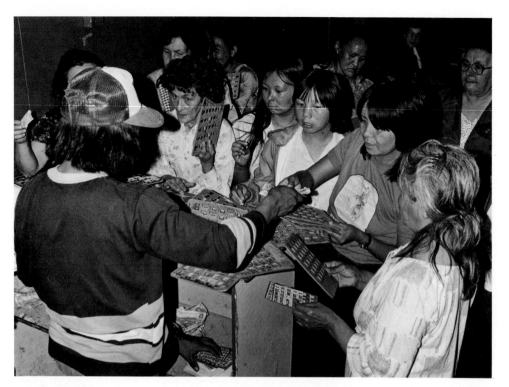

A game of bingo

Doris Onalik and child

William Onalik, repairing his boat below his house on the Hebron side of town, a resettlement area

Hopedale houses

Most Hopedale people are fishermen. They fish for about three months and after that it's unemployment. Some go trapping in the winter; those who have skidoos go hunting. Jobs are rare; you can hardly afford a new skidoo. I talk about skidoos because the caribou are around Nain and inside in the country. That's a long way from Hopedale.

I'm a weather observer year around. There are four of us taking eight-hour shifts. It's not paid well but better than no job at all.

Only the nurses' station, the teachers' residence, the school and the Mounties have running water. Most of our houses don't even have a bathroom. We have to fetch our water in buckets. The waste goes right out on the shore. No waste collection, just garbage once a week.

Here on the Hebron side, the houses are not insulated at all. When the temperature goes down to minus thirty we keep the stove on, day and night—use a forty-five gallon drum of stove oil every week. That's a lot of money to pay, and money is hard to come by.

Amos Onalik, Hopedale

Chesley Flowers, fixing his boat; in the background is the Mission's old gunpowder house.

Four, five generations back, my family came from England. No good asking me how they came. Maybe they were runaways.

I was doing a bit of sealing this spring, sixty-five by net. Sell the pelts, throw away the meat; no way to keep it.

When the American base came in here I worked for them for fourteen years. About eight years ago they left. There's only the drillers there now. They are drilling for oil sixty miles offshore. Some day they are going to have an oil leak. There wouldn't be too many birds and fish left.

Chesley Flowers, Hopedale

Harp seal skins

After having cut trees forty miles up the bay, the men skin the logs to build a fishermen's wharf.

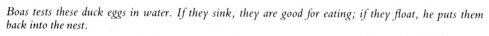

Boas tests these duck eggs in water. If they sink, they are good for eating; if they float, he puts them back into the nest.

Big companies come into Labrador and take out what they want, but we, who have always lived here, need to get a licence for food fishing, a licence for sealing, one for trapping, and another one for bird hunting. Pretty soon they will sell us a licence for berry picking, too.

Verona Winters, Hopedale

Boas Frieda with eider duck and drake

Every spring the capelin come to the shore to spawn. When they come like that we dip them with the dip net; you dip all you want. Now they are all out again in the deep water. The cod fish don't come in here no more. The water is too dirty. After we have a gale of wind the dirt comes up from the bottom.

There is salmon all around Hopedale from June to September, not quite as much as there used to be. After breakup, before the salmon comes in, we go way out into the bay, about forty-five miles, for trout. Some people call them trout, some call them char. We get all kinds: small ones and big ones, pink ones and red ones. We dry them in the sun for the winter. They dry quicker than the salmon; they are smaller. We keep the salmon too, but we pickle it in salt.

If we have seal, we slice them, put them on green sticks and dry them in the sun. Later we eat them just like that. We call them nipko. We got to get busy in the summer so we have enough food for the winter. If we want it, we can buy all kinds of meat in the government store.

Lots of people have no boat. They can't go anywhere. They have to borrow a boat from somebody to feed themselves. But if I know that a person needs a boat, I let them use it. Everybody is like that.

Joe Winters, Hopedale

Drying capelin

I've never been to school; just picked it up from the boats—the words, you know. We only speak Inuktut at home. I'm a settler, like my parents: part white, part Eskimo.

I'm eighty-one years old, born 1899, December ninth. Always out on the boat. You wouldn't believe all the fish I've got in my life, my young life. Never have trouble with my boat. Now those speedboats, those small boats, they are dangerous; lots of accidents now. But not the big ones. They just roll this way and that way, see? No trouble with them.

I don't fish any more. No, I'm too old. But when the *Bonavista* comes in, I'll be going up to Nain every week, come right back down, just for the ride. Every year I go on that boat, ride with the captain, eat with the crew— for free, you know.

I'd go on a boat any time; don't like them planes. It's faster all right, but who is in a hurry? And you can't catch no fish from the plane, you know; it's up too high.

Joe Abel, Hopedale

Joe Abel

The coastal boat Bonavista

The term up here is two years. For the single men that is a bit long. You can drive on the skidoo around the village only so many times before it starts getting boring, and you don't really ever get away from it all. We are on call twenty-four hours a day. We also have Davis Inlet, Postville and Makkovik to look after, and there are only five of us here in an area about the size of Germany. Each summer we like to have a man travel on the first run of the coastal boat, the *Bonavista*.

I am known as the old Mountie, having been here for two years. There is nobody over seventeen that I don't know by first name. I have lent people everything from boats to skidoos, skidoo parts, oil, gas, money, ammunition, guns, knives. It always comes back. I've been stung twice, that's all; just the younger crowd who want two dollars to go to the movies. Big money, it always comes back. And people come by and share the odd duck or goose or caribou. One of the big demands made on us is helping at income tax time. "Is so and so there?" "No, he's left." "Well, who is going to do my income tax this year? He did it last year; he got me seven hundred dollars back, and I want him again." People are allowed a lot of deductions, particularly the fishermen. They don't often keep receipts for their gas and boat motors and things they could claim later.

Some folk have the wrong idea about us altogether. We are here to help as much as we can. There are few of us who wouldn't come in if you invited us for coffee. We are policemen, but we are human too.

Eric Wheeler, detachment commander, RCMP Hopedale

Homeopathische Hausapotheke (homeopathic home pharmacy) dating back to the turn of the century

They are crazy, those Indians from Davis Inlet. They throw rocks at the *Bonavista* and they run around all day. We don't visit with them; they don't come here either. Inuit and Indians don't get along. We almost had war with them some time ago.

Verona Winters, Hopedale

Verona Winters at the museum in the old Mission building, Hopedale. She and Sybilla Nitsman have built an exhibit from the contents of boxes left by missionaries.

We are part of the Grenfell Mission, now known as the Grenfell Regional Health Service. They direct all health facilities for the northern Labrador coast out of North West River, including transporation of patients and staff.

"Is the Mission plane coming in today?" is a frequent question at the coast. Of course, when it is blowing forty- to sixty-mile winds, everything stays quiet—no flights come in, no boats go out. Should we have an emergency at the nursing station, we would look after that person until the plane is able to come in. Last week two babies were born here within a few hours of each other, both of them premature labour. Normally we send pregnant women out to North West River or Goose Bay for delivery.

Hopedale has approximately four hundred and fifty to five hundred people. It varies a lot, with visitors coming in, and fishermen going out for two or three months at a time, often taking along the entire family. For one year I had to do all the work by myself until we were able to get a public health nurse in. Nain has a resident doctor. She holds doctor's clinic in all the communities.

I love Hopedale and my friends here, but there are times in the winter when I do feel isolated—when no plane comes in, and no mail for two or three weeks at a time, and when one has to climb in and out of snowbanks to get from one building to the other. Quite a contrast to working in Zambia, where I had to travel long distances over hot, dry grasslands.

Ann McElligott, nurse-in-charge, Hopedale Nursing Station

Ann McElligott, meeting the Mission plane and its pilot, Tony Powell

The Moravian church, Nain

In some ways, Labrador people are privileged; we had more time to get used to the European system of settling in one place. The Moravian missionaries educated us to be commercial fishermen and showed us how to make use of the administrative structure. Most of us became Christians long before the people of the Northwest Territories. By the middle of the last century, most Labrador Inuit were able to read and write. In other ways this early contact was a drawback because we felt discrimination longer. But now we are threatened as never before. Legislation, bills and regulations are coming in continuously, challenging all the rights we are seeking. We have to watch that we don't form too many committees; if we are not careful, fishermen and hunters soon will become administrators.

One of our great concerns is the proposed hydro dam at the George River. We are so close to it. On our side of the river the climate will become moister and milder, according to research. That will affect the spawning of the char and the salmon, which are sensitive to temperature changes. We also know that the dam would upset the caribou migration. The caribou calve in Labrador and spend their winter in northern Quebec. Because the caribou is an animal whose instinct tells it to be here one season and over there the next, I don't know how long they would last if their pattern of migration were to be interfered with.

Because my whole family came from Hebron, I have a lot of things on my heart. In 1956 and 1959, the people from Nutak and Hebron were told to leave for other communities farther south. We were not given an option. They said, the church is moving, the store is moving, the medical facilities are moving, and we had no choice but to go. At that time there was an outbreak of tuberculosis, so naturally people were hesitant to stay. We were promised improved housing and services, but the government never kept its part of the bargain, and people are desperate to go back to their original places.

Every year our people go back to their original fishing camps, to the land they had to leave. The settlers are doing the same, and we are including them in our land claims. We still depend on our land and won't give it up.

Enoch Obed, land claims director, Labrador Inuit Association, Nain

I was born here in Nain. After my father died my mother remarried and we went to Hopedale. That's where I learned what I should know about life: how to work, fish, hunt. I got married there. It wasn't until I was thirty-nine years old that I started training as a minister at the Anglican Training School in Pangnirtung. Last year the Moravian Bishop from Ireland came and ordained me. I am the first Inuk minister ordained in the Moravian Church.

All the Inuit and settlers belong to the Moravian Church. The white people don't. They just work here for a while and leave again. The settlers are not really qalunaat. They are often mixed marriage; they are part of us.

Renatus Hunter, minister, Nain

Renatus Hunter, the first Inuk to become a minister of the Moravian Church of Labrador

The women's side of the church

The Moravian missionaries came from Herrnhut, Germany, in the eighteenth century. They translated all those beautiful songs in our hymnbook. Since they were also teaching school, we took over quite a few of their German words. Take for example the word "posauniti"; that's what we call a band. The trumpet is "posaunia" for the German Posaune, trombone. We pronounce all Biblical names the way the Germans do, since the Moravians translated the Bible from German into Inuktut. We say Jesaja, not Isaiah, Johannes, not John. My own name, Renatus, is Latin, "the one that is born again." I didn't know for a long time how beautiful a name I've got.

Renatus Hunter, minister, Nain

Tombstones at the cemetery in Nain

Clara Voisey with her new autoharp and her old family Bible

They say old Voisey was a cabin boy. He got so sick coming over from England, he wouldn't go back. That was Amos Voisey, my great-grand-father. His first wife was a native woman from Hopedale; after she died he married my great-grandmother, a native woman from Nain.

We are from Voisey Bay. There were fifteen of us in the family. For the first half of her children, my mother had my grandmother as a midwife. After grandmother died, this Inuit woman, Joe Finger's wife Joanna, was her midwife. In those days the Moravian minister came after Christmas by dog team. Sometimes he'd come after Easter too, anytime we had to be baptized. There were about thirty people living in the Bay.

We are related to just about every settler family. In every generation someone or other got married to a native woman, not so much to native men. All the settlers are pretty much related.

Clara Voisey, Nain

Michael Abele Atsatata and his wife Marie Debora, a well-known basket maker

Debora Atsatata: My father's name was Johannes Freitag, like Mittwoch, Donnerstag, Freitag.
Myself: That's German.
Debora: That's Inuktut, that's the way *we* say it.
Myself: How do you count?
Abele Atsatata: One, two, three . . .
Myself: But how do you count in Inuktut?
Abele: Eins, zwei, drei, viere, fuenfe, sechse, sieben, achte, neune, zehn.

My grandmother in Hebron made lots of potatoes. She knew how to make lots out of one potato. Kartupalak, that's what we call them.

Abele Atsatata, Nain

My daughter Sarah, when she lived in Baffin Island, asked a man to get her some kartupalaks. The language there is a little bit different from here. The man shook his head; he didn't understand. So she got out her last potato and showed it to him. That's not kartupalak, he said and laughed, that's pata-tees.

Bella Lyall, Nain

Henrietta Basto from Ramah, one of the old settlements on the northern Labrador coast

Bella Lyall

At the time of the Spanish flu in 1918 I was only six years old. We had all gone up sealing between Hebron and Okak. Our houses were small; it was just a camp. I remember staying with my aunt. I was not allowed in my father's house because people were starting to get sick and dying. I remember peeking into the window but I was not allowed in. My mother and my little baby sister died in there. They were the only ones that had a coffin. My father made it for them. One night my father brought me candy and a bottle of syrup. The next morning he too was dead. Nine of our people survived. Of the twenty-one Inuit who were there only two survived. I remember them shooting all the dogs because they went after the dead people who were left in my father's house. We kept our own dog team and went home, just leaving the place as it was. Later the house was broken down over the many bodies to be their grave. It's all grown over now; they say you can hardly make it out.

I am a true Labradorian, I think; I've lived here all my life. My grandparents were the Metcalfes; they'd come from England.

When I was young I learned to work hard. Later I did everything with my husband: set nets, hunted, trapped. We lived up there in the Bay, Tasiugak Bay—Tasiugak means "like a pond"—with another family there besides us. They were Inuit. If they got short of something, we helped them, or if they got fresh meat and things, they helped us. We worked and hunted and fished together and got along well. But since we moved here, you know, we don't mix with them as much as we did because now we have a different livelihood. My husband worked for the Hudson's Bay Company, for the Newfoundland government, and later, here, for the RCMP until he retired.

When I look back, I can say that we had a full and happy life.

Bella Lyall, Nain

Living in Nain is no good. Too far from the food. The seal is north, partridge, fox, hare—all good fishing is north.

Seventy-five schooners with fishermen came up to Nutak in 1946. Everyone went back with a full load to St. John's, and our small boats were full too.

July first, we'll leave, go north: Napartok Bay, Hebron, Ramah, Saglek. That's where the fish are, that's where the people are moving now. Stay all summer, never come back till September, October some time.

I will move back to Nutak one day, if we can have a nurse up there.

Abraham Zarpa, Nain

Lizzie Zarpa at her home

The commercial fishing season opens on July first and the boats leave to go north.

Abraham Zarpa, pulling in his net

Edward Martin Abele Zarpa

Lizzie Zarpa

I failed grade seven twice. I don't like failing school. Now I am fifteen, still in grade seven. I wished I were in grade eleven; I could go out to school, could go on the plane. I like walking in the water, and watching seals. I like going hunting, going on a speedboat. I like going dancing, but best of all I like to fish.

When I grow up I want to work at the hospital, or maybe at the fish plant.

Katie Zarpa, Nain

Katie Zarpa, fishing for char from the shore

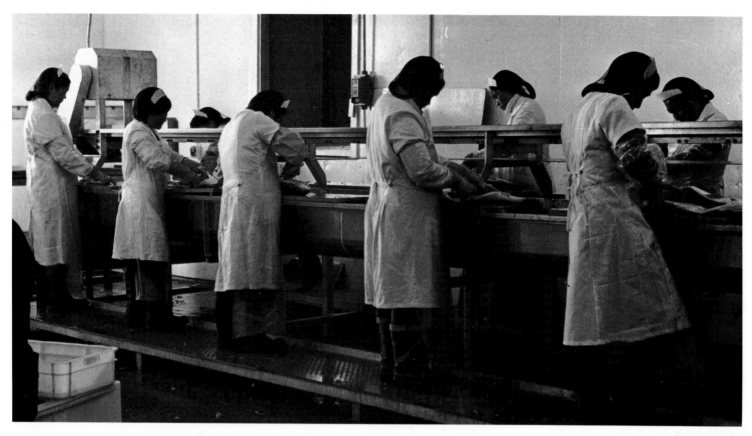

The fish plant is the only big employer in this town of nearly a thousand people, but the work is seasonal.

Arctic char, ready to be frozen

University Library
GOVERNORS STATE UNIVERSITY

Emilia Townley, carrying her water supply to her house

BEAUFORT SEA

HIGH ARCTIC

•Herschel Island

•BANKS ISLAND

•Sachs Harbour

Resolute Bay•

Tuktoyaktuk•   •McKinley Bay

Aklavik•

Mackenzie River•   •Inuvik   •Cape Parry   •Walker Bay

Parry Penisula   •Holman Island

WESTERN ARCTIC   Paulatuk•   •Brock River   CENTRAL ARCTIC

•Hornaday River

VICTORIA ISLAND•   BOOTHIA PENINSULA•

Coppermine•   Cambridge Bay•   Spence Bay•

Bay Chimo•   Gjoa Haven•   Pelly Bay

•Bathurst Inlet   Pelly Bay

•Back River

KEEWATIN

•Yellowknife   •Baker Lake

Kaminuriak Lake•

Chesterfield Inlet•
Rankin Inlet•
Kaminak Lake——•
Whale Cove•

Maguse Lake•
Eskimo Point•

•Churchill